FOOTBALL QUIZ BOOK

Football Quiz Book

Ian Thomson
and Mansel Davies

SPHERE BOOKS LIMITED

SPHERE BOOKS LTD

Published by the Penguin Group
27 Wrights Lane, London W8 5TZ, England
Viking Penguin Inc., 40 West 23rd Street, New York, New York 10010, USA
Penguin Books Australia Ltd, Ringwood, Victoria, Australia
Penguin Books Canada Ltd. 2801 John Street, Markham, Ontario, Canada L3R 1B4
Penguin Books (NZ) Ltd, 182–190 Wairau Road, Auckland 10, New Zealand

Penguin Books Ltd, Registered Offices: Harmondsworth, Middlesex, England

First published by Sphere Books Ltd 1988
10 9 8 7 6 5 4 3 2 1

Printed and bound in Great Britain by
Richard Clay Ltd, Bungay, Suffolk

1 *The 1987/88 Season*

1. Which player, just weeks before his transfer to a Division I club, scored four goals on the opening day of the 1987/1988 League season in Division III?

2. Who scored a First Division hat-trick in the space of four minutes, against Queen's Park Rangers, in December 1987?

3. Which famous club thrashed Everton 6–1 in August 1987, in a friendly match between respective national league champions?

4. Which Italian side struggled to defeat the Welsh representatives, Merthyr Tydfil, in the first round of the 1987/88 European Cup Winners' Cup, by an aggregate score of 3–2?

5. Who made his first full international appearance for Scotland in the European Championship qualifying match against Belgium in October 1987, six years after winning the last of his eight under-21 caps?

6. Who was the Heart of Midlothian midfield player who made his international début as a second-half substitute for Scotland against Bulgaria in Sofia, in November 1987, and scored the only goal of the match – a result which provided the Republic of Ireland with a place in the Finals of the 1988 European Championships?

7. Which country, playing at home, conceded four goals in the first twenty-four minutes of a European Championship qualifying match against England in November 1987?

8. Which club, in October 1987, became the first to register 6,000 goals in the Football League?

9. Which club, in November 1987, suffered its heaviest defeat in seventy-nine years of League football when Manchester City administered a 10–1 humiliation in their Division II match?

10. Who, after a fourteen-year association with the club, was sacked as manager in November 1987, just six months after leading his team to fifth place in Division I, their highest ever position in the Football League?

2 Football League Club Nicknames

1. Which famous team have the nickname 'The Red Devils'?

2. Which club answers to either 'The Baggies' or 'The Throstles'?

3. Which two Football League clubs are known as 'The Magpies'?

4. Which coastal clubs are identified as (a) 'The Seagulls', (b) 'The Mariners' and (c) 'The Seasiders'?

5. Where would the following be at home – (a) 'The Canaries', (b) 'The Owls', (c) 'The Blue Birds'?

6. Who are known as (a) 'The Lions' and (b) 'The Tigers'?

7. Which club are nicknamed 'The Trotters'?

8. Which clubs are known as (a) 'The Pilgrims' and (b) 'The Quakers'?

9. Which clubs are nicknamed (a) 'The Villains' and (b) 'The Valiants'?

10. Where are (a) 'The Bees' and (b) 'The Hornets'?

3 *The 1986 Mexico World Cup Finals*

1. Who celebrated his forty-first birthday by playing against Brazil in the 1986 World Cup, his 119th and final international appearance?

2. Who celebrated his thirty-first birthday by scoring the only goal that Brazil conceded during normal play in the 1986 World Cup finals?

3. Who was booked by the referee, for 'over celebrating', after scoring Scotland's only goal in the finals?

4. Which country gained an unexpected 1–0 victory over England in their opening game of the tournament?

5. Which England player was sent off against Morocco for throwing the ball at the referee?

6. Against which country did England score their first goals in the tournament, a hat-trick from Gary Lineker?

7. Who was the only England player other than Gary Lineker to score a goal during the finals?

8. Who was the English referee who took charge of the third-place play-off match between France and Belgium?

9. Who scored all three goals for the USSR in their 4–3 defeat by Belgium in round two, only the second time that a player scoring a hat-trick has finished on the losing side in the final stages of the World Cup?

10. Who equalled the World Cup record by scoring four goals in a match for Spain in their surprise 5–1 win over Denmark?

4 *Football League Division I – the 1980s*

1. Which club only retained their place in Division I at the end of the 1986/87 season by virtue of defeating Leeds United in a replay of their final match in the inaugural League play-off series?

2. Which club finished sixth in 1986/87, its first ever season in Division I of the Football League?

3. Which club won its first ten Division I games in the season 1985/86, but lost its opening three matches in 1986/87?

4. Which club succeeded in winning its final three League matches in the season 1984/85 to avoid being relegated from the First Division?

5. Which club won only three First Division matches and lost thirty-one in the season 1984/85?

6. Which club was relegated from the First Division in 1984/85 but won promotion the following season, duplicating the sequence it experienced between 1980 and 1982?

7. Which club achieved its highest ever League placing when finishing runners-up to Liverpool in the season 1983/84?

8. Which club, in its first season in Division I, finished runners-up in the League in 1982/83?

9. Which club finished third in Division I in the successive years 1981/82 and 1982/83, but slipped to fourth place for the next three seasons?

10. Which club finished First Division runners-up in the consecutive seasons 1980/81 and 1981/82?

5 *The European Cup – Goalscorers*

1. Who was the Barcelona reserve who scored a hat-trick against IFK Gothenburg in the semi-final of the 1986 European Cup, levelling the score in the tie at the end of the second leg?

2. Who scored the only goal of the 1982 European Cup final between Aston Villa and Bayern Munich?

3. Who scored the winning goal in a European Cup final in his first match in the competition?

4. Who is the only player to score for Liverpool in two European Cup finals?

5. Who scored Liverpool's goal in their 1–0 victory over Real Madrid in the 1981 European Cup final?

6. Who was the international centre-back who scored for Bayern Munich in the last minute of extra time in the 1974 European Cup final, earning a replay with Athletico Madrid?

7. Who scored both goals for Ajax in the 1972 European Cup final against Inter Milan?

8. Which player has scored for Celtic in two European Cup finals?

9. Who scored Partizan Belgrade's only goal in the 1966 European Cup final and Ajax's only goal in the 1969 final?

10. Who scored for Real Madrid in all their five successive European Cup final wins between 1956 and 1960?

6 *The FA Cup – Non-league Giant-killers*

1. Which club reached the third round of the FA Cup in 1986/87 for the first time in its history, taking Second Division Barnsley to a replay before losing by one goal to nil?

2. Which club beat Birmingham City, then a First Division side, at St Andrews, in the FA Cup third round in January 1986?

3. Which non-league club set a unique record when reaching the fourth round, and then the fifth round, of the FA Cup in successive seasons?

4. Which club were granted a replay by the FA after their goalkeeper had been knocked out by a lump of wood thrown from the crowd, when the score in their 1985 third-round tie with First Division Leicester City stood at one goal each?

5. Which side reached the fifth round of the FA Cup in 1978 with a 3–2 victory over Second Division Stoke City at the Victoria Ground?

6. Which side beat Leicester City, destined to be that season's Second Division champions, in a third-round replay in January 1980?

7. In 1975, which side followed up a third-round victory over First Division Burnley at Turf Moor by holding Leeds United to a goalless draw at Elland Road, before losing the replay, at Selhurst Park, to the only goal of the tie?

8. Which side beat Liverpool 2–1 in the third round in 1958/59?

9. Which side beat First Division Sunderland in the fourth round in 1949, before losing in the next round, 8–0 to Manchester United, at Maine Road, before a crowd of 81,565?

10. Which side beat First Division Newcastle United in a third-round replay in January 1972?

7 Current Football League Managers

1. Which manager guided his first club from the Fourth to the First Division of the Football League between 1983 and 1986?

2. Which former Northampton Town player managed the club to the championship of Division IV in the season 1986/87?

3. Which former player became manager of struggling Burnley in 1986, having previously held the position in 1979?

4. Which former West Ham United player has been manager of Bournemouth since October 1983?

5. Who, in his first managerial post, led Swindon Town from the Fourth Division to the Second Division in the successive seasons 1985/86 and 1986/87?

6. Who, after being forced to stop playing because of injury, was appointed manager of Crystal Palace in May 1984, at twenty-eight years of age?

7. Who was the successful manager of York City who took charge at Sunderland in May 1987?

8. Which mid-1960s Sheffield Wednesday player has been the manager of the club since June 1983?

9. Who, in July 1985, succeeded Lawrie McMenemy as manager of Southampton?

10. Which former Isthmian League player was appointed manager of Charlton Athletic in December 1982, guiding the club to the First Division in 1986 for the first time in twenty-nine years?

8 *Football League Transfers*

1. Which twenty-three-year-old was transferred in August 1984 for the fourth time in his career, bringing the aggregate fee to more than £3.6 million?

2. Who was the first player to be transferred between British clubs for a fee of £1.5 million (estimated)?

3. Who, in July 1980, became the second player to be transferred to Nottingham Forest for £1 million?

4. Who, in September 1979, was the first Scottish-born player to be transferred for more than £1 million?

5. Who, in January 1979, became the first player to be transferred between two British clubs for over £500,000, just one month before Trevor Francis was transferred for over £1 million?

6. Which player was both the first to be transferred between two Football League clubs for over £100,000, and the first for over £200,000?

7. Who was transferred twice within twelve months in 1968–69, on both occasions for record six-figure fees?

8. Who was transferred in November 1961 for a reputed £99,999?

9. Who, in 1960, was the first player to be transferred between two Football League clubs for more than £50,000?

10. Who, in 1977, became the first Irish-born player to be transferred for more than £100,000?

9 Mixed Bag

1. Which club was fined £4,500 by the FA in July 1987, when making its sixth successive annual appearance before the disciplinary commission?

2. Which former Chelsea centre-half and assistant manager of Southampton resigned as manager of Benfica in June 1987, after leading the club to the Portuguese League and Cup double?

3. Which Football League club decided, in 1987, to revert to a former name, last used in 1966?

4. Which two Scottish internationals left Celtic in June 1987 to join Nantes and Borussia Dortmund respectively?

5. Which two English internationals teamed up in July 1987 at Monaco?

6. Who was the former Bristol Rovers player-manager who joined Norwich City as a full-time player in 1985, and made his début for Wales, as a substitute against Saudia Arabia, in February 1986?

7. Which Tottenham Hotspur reserve goalkeeper replaced Ray Clemence for sixteen Football League matches in 1983/84, becoming a hero in the UEFA Cup Final, when he made two saves in the penalty-shoot-out victory over Anderlecht?

8. Which former Liverpool team-mate was signed by the Rangers manager, Graeme Souness, in May 1987?

9. Who, in September 1987, became England's 1,000th full international player when he replaced Glenn Hoddle during the second half of the 3–1 defeat by West Germany in Dusseldorf?

10. Who was given a free transfer in March 1986, after having been club captain since 1974?

10 England in the Final Stages of the World Cup

1. Who set a new World Cup record when he scored for England against France after just twenty-seven seconds of the opening group match in the 1982 tournament?

2. Who was included in England's final squad of twenty-two players for both the 1982 and 1986 World Cups, but was not called upon to participate in either tournament?

3. Who captained England in all their matches in the 1982 World Cup tournament?

4. Who replaced the indisposed Gordon Banks as England's goalkeeper for the 1970 World Cup quarter-final match with West Germany?

5. Who was replaced by Colin Bell during the second half of England's 1970 quarter-final with West Germany, in what proved to be his final international appearance?

6. Who, on his 1970 international début, scored with a penalty to give England a 1–0 win over Czechoslovakia which guaranteed a place in the quarter-finals?

7. Who scored the first goal conceded by Gordon Banks in the 1966 World Cup?

8. Who made his first appearance in the 1966 tournament at the quarter-final stage, when he replaced the injured Jimmy Greaves in the England team to meet Argentina?

9. Which country held England to a goal-less draw in their opening match of the 1966 tournament?

10. Who was the reigning Footballer of the Year who acted as coach to the 1962 England World Cup team in Chile?

11 *Goalscorers for England*

1. Who has scored a record forty-nine goals in an England career?

2. Who netted his nineteenth goal for England, in only his twenty-fourth international, when he opened the scoring against Brazil in the Rous Cup match at Wembley in May 1987?

3. Which winner of successive F A Cup losers' medals in 1897/98 and 1898/99 scored twenty-eight goals for England in just twenty-three international matches between 1895 and 1907?

4. Which teenage centre-forward, between October 1938 and May 1939, scored for England in each of his first six internationals?

5. Who scored a hat-trick for England on his début against Northern Ireland, in Belfast in September 1946, England's first international game after the Second World War?

6. Who made an auspicious début for England, with four goals against Portugal in a 10–0 victory in Lisbon, in May 1947?

7. Who was the Manchester United forward who scored six goals for England in six appearances between December 1948 and April 1952, including four in a game against Northern Ireland in November 1949?

8. Who scored seven goals for England in the 1960/61 home international championship – two against both Northern Ireland and Wales, and a further three in the 9–3 drubbing of Scotland?

9. Who scored ten goals for England in twelve appearances between October 1953 and October 1956, including four in the 7–2 win over Scotland in April 1955, so becoming the first England player to score a hat-trick against Scotland in eighty-three years of internationals?

10. Who, by scoring five goals for England against Cyprus in April 1975, became the first player to score five in a game for England since Tottenham Hotspur's Willie Hall in 1938, but had no further international success, and in fact made his final England appearance in the same year?

12 *The Inter-Cities Fairs Cup/European Fairs Cup/UEFA Cup – Clubs*

1. Which British club excelled with away victories against Barcelona and Borussia Moenchengladbach to reach the 1987 UEFA Cup Final?

2. Which was the last British club to win the UEFA Cup?

3. Which team of part-time players went through the 1981/82 UEFA Cup tournament undefeated, beating SV Hamburg in both legs of the final?

4. Which club, on winning the 1978 UEFA Cup final, became the third Dutch team to win a European competition?

5. Which club, from the Mediterranean island of Corsica, sprang a major surprise by reaching the final of the 1978 UEFA Cup competition?

6. Which club beat Ipswich on the 'away goals' rule in the first round of the 1974/75 UEFA Cup, and had the future Ipswich player, Frans Thijssen, in their team?

7. Which club won the European Fairs Cup in 1968, beginning a six-year run of victories by English sides?

8. Which British club reached the semi-final of the first Inter-Cities Fairs Cup, and the final of the next two?

9. Which club, managed by Jock Stein, lost by one goal to nil in a second-round play-off with the eventual competition winners, Valencia, in the 1962/63 Inter-Cities Fairs Cup?

10. Which club overcame Manchester United in a semi-final play-off before beating Juventus, in Turin, with the only goal of the 1965 Inter-Cities Fairs Cup final?

13 Scottish Football

1. Which Scottish club suffered its first home league defeat since May 1985 when it lost 5–2 to Rangers in February 1987?

2. Which Scottish league club now shares Firhill Park with Partick Thistle?

3. Which player-manager was sent off on the opening day of the 1986/87 Scottish league season in his first game for his new club, and suffered the same fate in May 1987, on the day his team made certain of winning the championship?

4. Which club joined the expanded Scottish league in 1974, and won the Division II championship for the first time in 1986/87?

5. Which club, who have never won the trophy, lost their fourth Scottish Cup final in fourteen years in 1987?

6. Who won a Scottish Cup winner's medal for Rangers against Celtic in 1973 and for Celtic against Rangers in 1977?

7. Which Celtic player retired in 1980, at the age of thirty-seven, after playing in 612 matches for the club, scoring 283 goals?

8. Who, between 1962 and 1978, made 496 league appearances for Rangers?

9. Which Scottish league club plays at a ground called Rugby Park?

10. Which club has won the Scottish league title just once, in 1931/32 – the only break in Celtic/Rangers domination between 1904 and 1947?

14 Football League – Leading Club Goalscorers

1. Which player, between 1978 and 1986, scored a club record 129 League goals in a career for Bury, before being transferred to West Bromwich Albion?

2. Who scored 151 League goals for Leeds United between 1965 and 1979, and a further 17 between 1983 and 1986 on his return to the club, which took him past John Charles's career record of 154 goals for the club?

3. Who scored 155 goals for Southampton between 1966 and 1976 and a further 27 on his return to the club in 1979, taking him beyond Terry Paine's career record of 160 goals for the club?

4. Who scored 164 League goals in 302 games for Chelsea between 1958 and 1970, surpassing Jimmy Greaves's record of 157 goals during the 1968/69 season ?

5. Who scored a total of 154 League goals for his club in two spells, from 1966 to 1978 and 1980 to 1982, having previously scored 113 League goals for Bradford Park Avenue?

6. Who scored 349 League goals for Everton between 1925 and 1937, a record total for one English League club?

7. Who scored 315 goals for Bristol City in 597 League matches between 1951 and 1966?

8. Which South African-born player, also a Kent cricketer, scored 153 goals for Charlton Athletic, in 376 League appearances between 1953 and 1962?

9. Who scored 243 goals in 406 League games for Luton Town between 1950 and 1964?

10. Who scored 326 League goals for Middlesbrough between 1925 and 1939?

15 *Family Connections*

1. Who were the two brothers who played for Manchester United in the 1977 FA Cup Final?

2. Who were the twins who both played in the 1967 League Cup final?

3. Who were the twins, one a centre-half and the other a centre-forward, who played together for Chester, Luton Town and Manchester City between 1974 and 1978?

4. Who are the two brothers who both won international caps in the 1960s, the elder playing eleven times for Wales, and the younger once for England?

5. Who were the last father and son to play football for England?

6. Who are the father and son who have both managed Fulham since the Second World War?

7. Which two brothers managed clubs that won League championships during the 1960s, one in Scotland and the other in England?

8. Which pair of brothers, sons of a footballing father, both played more than 100 League games for Chelsea during the 1970s?

9. Which father of a current England international forward scored more than 200 League goals, in a fifteen-year career with eight different clubs?

10. Who are the father and son who respectively won thirty and fifty-one caps for Eire, the father being principally remembered as a centre-half with Aston Villa in the years immediately after the Second World War, and the son for playing nearly 150 League games for Newcastle United after transferring from West Bromwich Albion in 1978?

16 *Northern Ireland Internationals*

1. Who won fifty-six caps for Northern Ireland between October 1949 and November 1962, becoming the first player to make more than fifty appearances for his country?

2. Who, between May 1951 and November 1963, made fifty-six appearances for Northern Ireland, whilst playing with Sunderland, Luton Town, Everton and Port Vale?

3. Which current Northern Ireland international made his début for his country in February 1972, at the age of seventeen years and six months?

4. Which Linfield centre-forward, in February 1930, scored six goals against Wales in a 7–0 victory in Belfast?

5. Which greatly admired Northern Ireland footballer won sixteen international caps between February 1935 and November 1950, whilst playing for Blackpool, Manchester City, Derby County, Huddersfield Town and Doncaster Rovers?

6. Who, between 1976 and 1986, won twenty-three caps for Northern Ireland, as understudy goalkeeper to Pat Jennings?

7. Who was the goalkeeper, hero of the Munich air crash, who played twenty-five times for Northern Ireland between 1954 and 1964?

8. Which twenty-nine-year-old forward, who made forty-one appearances for Northern Ireland between 1978 and 1986, was forced to retire at the age of twenty-nine with a recurring knee injury?

9. Who, at the age of seventeen, succeeded the veteran Billy Bingham, when he made his Northern Ireland début against Wales in April 1964, making his thirty-seventh and final appearance in October 1978?

10. Which Arsenal and Hull City central defender played fifty-nine times for Northern Ireland between 1961 and 1973, a record later surpassed by Pat Jennings?

17 *World Cup—Mixed Bag*

1. Who, in 1978, became the first substitute to score in the World Cup Final?

2. Who came on as substitute for Italy in the 1982 World Cup Final after just seven minutes of play, scored his country's third goal, and was himself substituted two minutes before the end of the match?

3. Who came on as a substitute for Brazil against France in the 1986 World Cup tournament and immediately had to take a penalty, which was saved by the goalkeeper?

4. Who, in 1978, scored the thousandth goal in World Cup tournaments, when he beat Scotland's goalkeeper, Alan Rough, from the penalty spot?

5. Who scored a penalty for Holland in the first minute of the 1974 World Cup Final?

6. Who scored four penalties during the 1966 World Cup finals, and finished as the tournament's leading scorer with nine goals?

7. Which goalkeeper played for more than 400 minutes in the 1982 World Cup tournament without conceding a goal?

8. Who was Holland's goalkeeper in both the 1974 and 1978 World Cup Finals?

9. Who is the only goalkeeper to gain two World Cup winner's medals?

10. Which goalkeeper is the only footballer to play in five World Cup tournaments?

18 *The FA Cup – Clubs*

1. Which club, in February 1987, ended Everton's attempt to reach a fourth successive FA Cup final with a convincing 3–1 fifth-round victory?

2. Which was the last club before Everton to play in three successive FA Cup finals?

3. Which was the last club to play in the FA Cup final and be relegated from the First Division in the same season?

4. Which was the last Second Division club to appear in the FA Cup final?

5. Which club has played in four post-war FA Cup finals and lost them all?

6. Which is the only club to have won the FA Cup by overcoming First Division opposition in every round?

7. Which club has appeared in four FA Cup finals, all of which have featured a Second Division club?

8. Which club won the FA Cup for the only time in its history in 1911, by coincidence just a few months after the current trophy was manufactured in that city?

9. Which was the first club to play in successive Wembley FA Cup finals?

10. Which club won the FA Cup on seven occasions before suffering its first defeat in a final?

19 *Transfer Trail – England Internationals*

Identify the subject of the following transfer deals – in each case the answer is an England international and brief details of his international career are appended:

1. (25 caps September 1977 – June 1982)
   February 1972   Bury to Newcastle United   £25,000

2. (4 caps March 1976 – May 1976)
   October 1973   Southend United to Crystal Palace £120,000

3. (49 caps February 1966 – April 1972)
   August 1975   Stoke City to West Bromwich Albion £20,000

4. (11 caps May 1981 – November 1984)
   August 1975   Wolverhampton Wanderers to Birmingham City   £50,000

5. (6 caps November 1981 – November 1982)
   February 1976 Preston North End to Burnley £100,000

6. (13 caps June 1985 – June 1988)
   June 1979 Nottingham Forest to Queen's Park Rangers   £235,000

7. (4 caps April 1974 – May 1974)
   September 1979   Everton to Aston Villa   £250,000

8. (8 caps October 1974 – November 1975)
   October 1979   Everton to Wolverhampton Wanderers   £325,000

9. (2 caps May 1975)
   March 1980   Manchester City to Chelsea   £60,000

10. (5 caps April 1974 – February 1977)
    July 1980   Nottingham Forest to Orient   £100,000

20 1987—Mixed Bag

1. Which former Newport County manager was dismissed as coach to the Spanish club, Real Celta, in August 1987, having led them to promotion, but was immediately back in the game when he resumed a position in the Football League which he had last held ten years before?

2. Who is the young Stoke City defender who has a 'pacemaker' to overcome a heart defect?

3. Who scored for Newcastle United in seven successive Football League matches in March and April 1987, so equalling a post-war club record?

4. Which former England international goalkeeper was forced to retire from the game in April 1987, at twenty-eight years of age, owing to a recurring knee injury?

5. Which former England international scored for Merthyr Tydfil in their 1986/87 Welsh Cup Final victory over Newport County?

6. Who was the twenty-nine-year-old captain of Leicester City who made his international début for Scotland against England, in the goalless Rous Cup encounter at Hampden Park in May 1987?

7. Which club won the 1986/87 Freight Rover Trophy, the first Wembley cup final to be decided on penalties?

8. Which young Manchester United player was sent off after just eighty-five seconds of the First Division match at Southampton in January 1987?

9. Which Scottish club surprisingly defeated the champions elect, Glasgow Rangers, at Ibrox in the third round of the 1986/87 Scottish FA Cup, full-back Adrian Sprott scoring a second-half goal to give them a 1–0 victory?

10. Which goalkeeper established a new British record of 1,196 minutes without conceding a goal during the 1986/87 season, beating a record previously set by Aberdeen's Bobby Clark in 1970/71?

21 *The Football League Cup*

1. Which Third Division side caused probably the biggest upset in a League Cup final by beating Arsenal 3–1, after extra time, in 1969?

2. Which club in 1965 became the first to play in two consecutive League Cup finals?

3. Who scored all five goals for Southampton in their 5–4 victory over Leeds United in the fourth round of the 1960/61 League Cup competition?

4. Who scored eleven goals for Aston Villa in the inaugural League Cup competition in 1960/61, in spite of being transferred before the final?

5. Who scored four goals for Queen's Park Rangers in a first-round tie against Colchester United in 1966/67, and again against Tranmere Rovers in the third round in 1969/70?

6. Which two clubs contested a League Cup final which required two replays to produce a result?

7. Which former Football League secretary nurtured the idea of the League Cup?

8. Which manager led both Aston Villa and Manchester City to their first League Cup final successes?

9. Which thirty-five-year-old scored the winning goal for Stoke City in the 1972 League Cup final, and subsequently succeeded Tony Waddington as the club manager?

10. Who scored the only goal in the 1980 League Cup final between Wolverhampton Wanderers and Nottingham Forest?

22 *The European Cup Winners' Cup – Players*

1. Who scored all Everton's three goals in their quarter-final home leg against Fortuna Sittard in 1984/85?

2. Who was the substitute who scored Aberdeen's winning goal, six minutes before the end of extra time, in the 1983 final?

3. Who was the only outfield player not to score for Liverpool when nine of the team netted in an 11–0 home victory over Stromgodset of Norway, in the 1974/75 first round?

4. Who scored two goals for Anderlecht in both the 1976 and 1978 finals?

5. Who missed Arsenal's sixth spot-kick to give Valencia a 5–4 victory on penalties in the 1980 final?

6. Which British player ended up as the leading goalscorer in the European Cup Winners' Cup in 1971/72, scoring all his eight goals in a first-round tie against Jeunesse Hautcharage of Luxemburg?

7. Who scored for Barcelona in both the 1969 and 1979 finals?

8. Who scored both West Ham United's goals in the 1965 final?

9. Which players scored Manchester City's two goals in the 1970 final?

10. Who scored two goals for Rangers in their 1972 final victory in Barcelona?

23 *Football League Clubs – Division II*

1. Which club won promotion from Division II in the season 1986/87, after finishing fourth, just out of the promotion places, in the previous two seasons?

2. Which club, in finishing third in Division II in the season 1986/87, achieved its best League position since being relegated from Division I in 1923?

3. Which club was relegated to the Third Division for the first time in its history at the end of the 1986/87 season?

4. Which club won promotion from the Second Division for the first time ever in 1984/85?

5. Which club, after just fourteen years as members of the Football League, won only four League matches in 1983/84, so bringing to an end a run of six successive seasons in Division II?

6. Which club was promoted to Division I in 1984/85 after just one season in Division II, thereby repeating its achievement of 1979/80?

7. Which club won the Second Division championship with the second-best ever total of sixty-six points in 1980/81?

8. Which club won the Second Division championship four times between 1953/54 and 1979/80?

9. Which Second Division club, in six seasons from 1955/56 to 1960/61, when only the first two teams were promoted, finished third in the table on four occasions and fourth twice, before winning the championship in 1961/62?

10. Which was the last club before Ipswich Town in 1960/61 and 1961/62 to win the Second Division championship and the First Division title in successive seasons?

24 The European Championships

1. Which country won the 1984 European Championships in Paris?

2. Who scored nine goals in five matches, including two hat-tricks, in the course of the 1984 tournament?

3. Which UK nation failed to qualify for the finals in 1984 because Yugoslavia scored a last-minute winning goal against Bulgaria?

4. Who scored seven goals for England in their qualifying matches for the 1980 European Championships, more than anyone else in the competition, but failed to score in the three tournament group games?

5. Who scored both West Germany's goals in the 1980 final against Belgium?

6. Who was the thirty-five-year-old midfield general who helped to inspire Belgium to reach the 1980 European Championship Final?

7. Which country took the 1976 European Championships, winning a penalty shoot-out after extra time?

8. Who scored eleven goals in ten matches during the 1972 tournament?

9. Which little-regarded football-playing country held West Germany to a goalless draw in the 1968 European Championships, so preventing the favourites from qualifying for the quarter-finals?

10. Which country beat England 5–2 in 1963, in the second leg of a first-round match in what was then the European Nations' Cup – Alf Ramsey's first game as the England team manager?

25 England Players

1. Who made two England appearances, both in October 1959, against Wales and Sweden, being Billy Wright's immediate successor as England centre-half?

2. Who made his only two England appearances at centre-forward in the same two 1959 games against Wales and Sweden, but failed to score in either match?

3. Who made sixty-five appearances for England between 1974 and 1982, while playing for five different clubs – the only player prior to Peter Shilton in 1987 to be capped while at so many clubs?

4. Who was just nineteen years old when he made his England début, as a substitute against Northern Ireland in May 1983, coincidentally seven years to the day after England's previous teenager, Ray Wilkins, made his international début?

5. Which current First Division player made his only appearance for England in April 1974?

6. Which other Bolton-born centre-forward exceeded Nat Lofthouse's thirty-three caps for England when he played against East Germany at Wembley in September 1984?

7. Which Liverpool player, in his second international appearance, against Switzerland in June 1963, scored in an 8–1 victory but was never selected for his country again?

8. Which Liverpool player's second game for England was in the 1966 World Cup tournament, against France, his third game being against Switzerland in September 1977?

9. Who has played for England over a record period of twenty-two years and 228 days?

10. Who was the only player to appear both in England's last official international match before the Second World War, against Rumania in Bucharest in May 1939, and in their first post-war match, against Northern Ireland in Belfast seven years later?

26 Scotland in the Final Stages of the World Cup

1. Which Scottish footballer was omitted from the squad of twenty-two players for the 1986 World Cup tournament, despite travelling to Melbourne in December 1985, and playing in the final qualifying match against Australia?

2. Which Scottish footballer is the only United Kingdom player who has scored in three different World Cup tournaments?

3. Which country lost 5–2 to Scotland in the 1982 tournament?

4. Which country went on to play in a World Cup Final after losing to Scotland in an earlier group match?

5. Who missed a penalty for Scotland against Peru in their opening game of the 1978 tournament, was almost immediately substituted, and never played for his country again?

6. Who played his fifty-fifth and final international match for Scotland in their opening game of the 1974 tournament against Zaïre?

7. Who became Scotland's first ever World Cup tournament substitute when he replaced Kenny Dalglish in the match against Zaïre in 1974?

8. Which country brought Scotland's first World Cup venture to an abrupt end with a 7–0 victory in 1954?

9. Who played for Scotland in the 1954 tournament and was team manager in the 1974 tournament?

10. Who became the first Scotland player to score two goals in a World Cup match when he converted after a brilliant individual dribble and also scored from a penalty in their final group game in 1978?

27 British Club Grounds

1. Which Fourth Division club shares the same ground name as Newcastle United?

2. Which League ground accommodated 84,569 spectators for a sixth-round FA Cup tie in March 1934?

3. Which two English League clubs are both at home on the Recreation Ground?

4. Which two English League clubs have home advantage at the County Ground?

5. Which Scottish Division II club plays at Annfield Park?

6. Which Scottish clubs play at Fir Park and Firhill Park?

7. Which English Football League ground hosted Northern Ireland's home game against England in May 1973?

8. Which two English League clubs play at home at the Victoria Ground?

9. In which English town would you find Blundell Park?

10. Which Scottish Division II club plays at Hampden Park?

28 Football League—Mixed Bag

1. Who was the sixteen-year-old who scored all his side's four goals in a Division II game in February 1971?

2. Which England international made his League début as a sixteen-year-old for Reading against Mansfield Town in a Third Division game in February 1980?

3. Who made his League début for Manchester United against Cardiff City at Old Trafford on Easter Monday 1953, at the age of fifteen years and 285 days?

4. Who was fifty-one years and four months old when he played in goal for New Brighton against Hartlepool in a Third Division North match in March 1947?

5. Who was fifty years and five days old when he played his last game for Stoke City in February 1965, becoming the oldest outfield player to appear in a first-class match?

6. Who saved a penalty for Birmingham City in December 1980, with his first touch of the ball in his first League match?

7. Who was the Ipswich Town goalkeeper who saved eight of the ten penalties he faced in First Division games in the season 1979/80?

8. Which team missed a penalty in its last League match of the season and, as a consequence, was pipped for the League championship?

9. Which club did not register a League victory in the Fourth Division in 1970/71 until its twenty-sixth game, but then won nine of its final twenty matches, ending the season third from bottom?

10. Who scored six goals on his début for Newcastle United, in a 13–0 Second Division win over Newport County in October 1946?

29 *The FA Cup – Players*

1. Which Coventry City player was forced to miss the 1987 FA Cup Final when he underwent a knee operation the day before the match?

2. Who was called up to play for Liverpool in the 1986 FA Cup Final as a late replacement for the injured Gary Gillespie?

3. Who was the Watford captain who missed the 1984 FA Cup Final through suspension, after being sent off in a League match at Luton?

4. Who was the Queen's Park Rangers captain who played in the first game of the 1982 FA Cup Final against Tottenham Hotspur, but was not available for the replay because of suspension?

5. Who, in 1978, became only the second man to be sent off in an FA Cup semi-final, forty-eight years after Arthur Childs had suffered the same fate when playing for Hull City against Arsenal?

6. Who scored for Nottingham Forest in the 1959 FA Cup Final, but had to go off later suffering a broken shin-bone, and watched the end of the match on a hospital television?

7. Which current player, at the age of twenty-three, became the youngest FA Cup winning captain since Bobby Moore in 1964?

8. Who captained Manchester United in three FA Cup Finals between 1976 and 1979?

9. Who was the Welsh international who captained Manchester City in successive FA Cup Finals in 1955 and 1956?

10. Who captained Bolton Wanderers in the first FA Cup Final at Wembley in 1923, again in 1926, when Bolton won at Wembley for a second time, and was subsequently to manage Blackpool in three FA Cup Final appearances between 1948 and 1953?

30 *Mixed Bag*

1. Which holder of the most international caps for Wales made his seventy-second and final appearance for his country in May 1986, against Canada in Toronto?

2. Who scored a record thirteen penalty goals in a season in Football League games in 1971/72?

3. Who became the first teenager to be transferred for £100,000, moving from Wolverhampton Wanderers to Liverpool in September 1968?

4. Which are the only two clubs in the Football League, never to have been relegated?

5. Which Third Division club lost 2–0 at home to Leeds United in the quarter-final of the 1986/87 FA Cup, having never previously progressed beyond the last thirty-two in the competition?

6. Who was the South Wales wine-bar owner, and former Newport County goalkeeper, who received a surprise call to play for Watford in the 1986/87 FA Cup semi-final match against Tottenham Hotspur at Villa Park?

7. Who set the original record of nineteen goals in matches between Liverpool and Everton, which was equalled by Ian Rush in April 1987?

8. Which Football League Division I club dismissed two managers during the 1986/87 season?

9. Which member of Coventry City's 1987 FA Cup winning team had played in a previous FA Cup Final against Tottenham Hotspur?

10. Who was voted Scottish Footballer of the Year for 1986/87, his first season north of the border?

31 *Welsh Internationals*

1. Who was the Port Vale forward who won his first cap for Wales in April 1987, replacing the suspended Mark Hughes, and scored in a 4–0 victory over Finland at Wrexham?

2. Who was the centre-forward from Third Division Chester who scored four goals for Wales in a 7–0 victory over Malta in October 1978?

3. Who scored a hat-trick for Wales in a 3–0 victory over Scotland at Cardiff in May 1979?

4. Which much-transferred forward from North Wales appeared in thirty-four international matches between October 1963 and September 1973, whilst playing for five different Football League clubs?

5. Who, between November 1950 and May 1966, played sixty-eight times for Wales, scoring twenty-two goals?

6. Who was switched from his more usual defensive role to score all four goals for Wales against Northern Ireland, in Cardiff in April 1962?

7. Who has been Wales's most prolific scorer to date, with twenty-three goals in thirty-eight appearances between October 1946 and October 1956?

8. Who was the Swansea forward who scored a hat-trick against East Germany in September 1957, in the second of his three appearances?

9. Who made his forty-eighth and final appearance for Wales in March 1920, against England at Highbury, at the age of forty-five years and eight months?

10. Which centre-forward, at the age of eighteen years and seven months, scored for Wales on his début in October 1959, in the 1–1 draw with England which was played at his club ground, Ninian Park?

32 World Cup—Mixed Bag

1. Which country has lost a record seventeen of the twenty-nine matches that it has played in nine World Cup tournaments?

2. Which country has played in every tournament between 1930 and 1986?

3. Which country won the World Cup on the only occasion that the tournament was played in Brazil?

4. Which country scored in a World Cup Final before any of the opposition players had touched the ball?

5. Which country won a World Cup Final despite being two goals down after just eight minutes of play?

6. Which country has played sixteen matches in five World Cup tournaments, yet has not won any of them?

7. Which country failed to make the semi-final of the 1982 tournament, despite conceding just one goal, and that goal scored in a game that they won?

8. Which country beat West Germany in a first-phase match of the 1982 tournament?

9. Which country used all its twenty-two squad players over three matches in the 1978 World Cup, and, in both the 1982 and 1986 tournaments, played every squad member except the third-choice goalkeepers?

10. Which country withdrew from the 1950 tournament following a FIFA ruling that its team would not be allowed to play in bare feet?

33 *Football League Clubs – Mixed Bag*

1. Which club was fined £10,000 in July 1987 for fielding a mainly reserve side in its last League match of the 1986/87 season?

2. Which club, managed by Sir Stanley Matthews, was expelled from the Football League in 1968 for financial irregularities, but re-elected for the following season?

3. Which Third Division club, found guilty of offering illegal bonuses, was fined £500 and had nineteen points deducted to enforce relegation to the Fourth Division at the end of the 1967/68 season?

4. Which First Division club had its ground closed at the start of the 1971/72 season following a pitch invasion the previous April in protest at a disputed offside goal?

5. Which club finished runners-up in the Football League championship in four of the first five seasons after the Second World War, before winning the title in 1951/52?

6. Which club lost its League status in 1978, being replaced by Wigan Athletic?

7. Which was the last southern-based club, prior to Newport County, to lose its League status, deciding not to apply for re-election in 1932?

8. Which club joined the Football League in the Third Division South in 1938/39, and has since won both the League championship and the FA Cup?

9. Which Division I club suffered its record home defeat on Boxing Day 1963, 8–2 to Blackburn Rovers, but two days later took revenge with a 3–1 win at Blackburn?

10. Which club handed Liverpool their worst League defeat, with a 9–1 win in a Division II game in December 1954?

34 *The European Cup – Clubs*

1. Which club lost the 1986 European Cup Final in a penalty shoot-out, having put out IFK Gothenburg on penalties in the semi-final?

2. Which British club was forced by UEFA to play its European Cup first-round home leg against Besiktas behind closed doors, part of the punishment for the crowd trouble during the previous season's semi-final tie against Anderlecht in Brussels?

3. Which British club suffered successive first-round eliminations from the European Cup in 1978/79 and 1979/80?

4. Which was the second club, after Real Madrid, to win the European Cup at the first attempt?

5. Who won two European Cup winner's medals, fourteen years apart, but only played for a total of eight minutes in the two finals?

6. Which club defeated five-times winners, Real Madrid, by an aggregate score of four goals to three in the first round of the 1960/61 competition?

7. Which club, in 1961, succeeded Real Madrid as the European Cup winners?

8. Which British club beat Anderlecht by ten goals to nil in its first home game in the European Cup?

9. Which was the only British team in the inaugural European Cup competition in 1955/56?

10. Which team, in June 1956, played Real Madrid in Paris, in the first ever European Cup Final?

35 *Football League Transfers*

1. Who was transferred for £1.9 million in July 1987, a record fee between two Football League clubs?

2. Who was transferred for £850,000 in July 1987, a record fee for a player moving from Scotland to England?

3. Who, in September 1979, became the first uncapped player to be transferred for more than £1 million?

4. Which Worcester City defender set a record in December 1978 for the most expensive non-League transfer, when Everton paid £30,000 for his services?

5. Who became the first full-back to be transferred between Football League clubs for £100,000, when he moved in August 1970 from Sheffield Wednesday to Coventry City?

6. Who, in October 1950, became the first player to be transferred for £30,000, when he moved from Aston Villa to Sunderland?

7. Who, in February 1979, became the first goalkeeper to be transferred for more than £500,000?

8. Who was transferred from Wolverhampton Wanderers to Arsenal for £14,000 in 1938, the highest pre-war transfer fee?

9. Who, in 1928, became the first player to command a five-figure transfer fee, when he moved from Bolton Wanderers to Arsenal for £10,890?

10. Who, in 1905, became the first player to be transferred for £1,000, when he moved from Sunderland to Middlesbrough?

36 *England Caps*

1. Who, at Hampden Park in 1959, became the first footballer to play 100 games for England?

2. Who was the Blackburn Rovers full-back who set a record by playing forty-two times for England, between 1901 and 1914?

3. Who played in England's last five international matches before the start of the Second World War, made twenty-seven appearances in wartime and Victory internationals, but was never selected for a post-war international, despite remaining one of the First Division's most influential players until his retirement in 1954?

4. Who was the only member of England's 1966 World Cup Final team to make fewer than thirty international appearances?

5. Who appeared in just thirteen matches for England, making his début as a twenty-year-old in April 1934 and playing his last game, thirteen years later, in May 1947?

6. Who was the first player to appear for England after having signed for a continental club?

7. Who won thirty-five caps for England between November 1955 and May 1960, and succeeded Billy Wright as team captain in October 1959?

8. Who was England's goalkeeper in their first seventeen post-war internationals, between September 1946 and November 1948, replaced by Ted Ditchburn for the 6–0 victory over Switzerland in December 1948?

9. Who was the last player to represent England in three different decades, winning his first cap against the Netherlands in November 1969, and his last against Scotland in May 1980?

10. Who, after twenty-seven consecutive appearances as England's centre-half, ended his international career in April 1950 when he signed a contract to play for a Colombian club?

37 *West Germany in the World Cup*

1. Which West German goalkeeper, after Holland's first-minute penalty in the 1974 final, played a further 475 minutes of World Cup football before conceding another goal?

2. Which country beat West Germany by one goal to nil in Stuttgart in October 1985, the first time that the West Germans have ever lost a World Cup qualifying game?

3. Who scored five goals for West Germany in the 1982 World Cup but only managed to score once in the 1986 competition?

4. Who became only the third player to score in two World Cup Finals, when he shot West Germany's 'consolation' goal against Italy in 1982?

5. Who was the only West German to play in both the World Cup Finals of 1966 and 1974, in addition to the third-place play-off in 1970?

6. Who concluded his World Cup career in 1974 with West Germany's deciding goal in the final – his fourteenth in thirteen matches, spread over two tournaments?

7. Who scored for West Germany in the 1966 World Cup quarter-final, semi-final and final?

8. Who scored West Germany's last-minute equalizer against Italy in the semi-final of the 1970 World Cup – his only goal in the competition, in his fourth World Cup tournament?

9. Which country, playing West Germany for the first time in an international, inflicted the only defeat on the eventual champions in the 1974 tournament?

10. Who were the brothers who won World Cup winners medals for West Germany in the 1954 tournament?

38 Football League—Mixed Bag

1. Which secretary of the Professional Footballers' Association negotiated the abolition of the players' maximum wage?

2. Which League footballer was reported to be the first £100-a-week club professional?

3. Which former winger, who spent most of his playing career with Bolton Wanderers and Birmingham City, is the current Secretary of the Professional Footballers' Association?

4. Who, between 1974 and 1984, successively managed both the north London giants, Tottenham Hotspur and Arsenal?

5. Who spent the early years of his Football League career at Oxford and Cambridge, playing for Oxford United and later managing Cambridge United?

6. Which former international player and manager was known in his playing days as the 'General'?

7. Which current television personality had the nickname 'Crazy Horse', because of his enthusiastic, and arguably uncoordinated-looking, style of play?

8. Which loyal club player and unpretentious 'hard man' was appropriately, but affectionately, nicknamed 'Chopper'?

9. Which former England midfield player, renowned for his tireless running, was called 'Nijinsky' by his teammates?

10. Who was the ball-juggling entertainer and crowd-puller at Roker Park who became known as the 'Clown Prince of Soccer'?

39 *The European Championships*

1. Which country qualified ahead of England for the 1984 European Championships after winning by a goal to nil at Wembley?

2. Which country won its final qualifying game for the 1984 European Championships 12–1, when it required victory by an eleven-goal margin to qualify ahead of Holland?

3. Which UK nation beat West Germany both home and away in the qualifying games for the 1984 European Championships, but could not prevent them from going through to the tournament's final stages?

4. Which country beat Denmark by five penalties to four to qualify for the 1984 European Championship final?

5. Which former European Footballer of the Year broke his leg against France in his country's opening game at the 1984 European Championships?

6. Who was the only member of West Germany's 1976 European Championship final team also to play in the 1980 final?

7. Who scored all West Germany's three goals against Holland in the 1980 group one match, helping to ensure his country's place in the final?

8. Which country won seven out of eight qualifying matches for the 1980 European Championships, scoring twenty-two goals in the process, and conceding only five?

9. In which European Championships did both semi-final matches, the third-place play-off and the final itself all go to extra time?

10. In which European Championships did England finish third, the best result achieved to date by a UK nation?

40 *Football League Goalscorers*

1. Who, playing for Reading in their Fourth Division match against Stockport County in September 1983, scored three goals in four minutes and twelve seconds, the third-fastest hat-trick in the history of the Football League?

2. Which Sunderland player scored his twentieth consecutive penalty, over a six-year period, when the Wearsiders beat Liverpool at Anfield in October 1983?

3. Who, in August 1983, scored both goals for Manchester United, the FA Cup holders, in their 2–0 Charity Shield victory over Liverpool – the first outright win by FA Cup holders since Tottenham Hotspur had beaten Ipswich Town 5–1 in 1962?

4. Who scored five goals in a fifty-minute period at Villa Park in October 1983, helping his club to defeat Aston Villa 6–2?

5. Which sixteen-year-old schoolboy became the youngest goalscorer in a First Division match in February 1984, when he helped Ipswich Town to register a 3–1 victory over Coventry City?

6. Who scored for Liverpool against West Ham United in August 1984, just fourteen seconds into his Anfield début?

7. Who scored a total of ten goals for Liverpool on three successive Saturdays in November 1946, recording First Division hat-tricks against Portsmouth, Derby County and Arsenal?

8. Which full-back scored ten League goals for his club, all from open play, in the 1969/70 First Division programme?

9. Which full-back scored more than seventy League goals in his career, including thirty-four for Southampton between 1974 and 1980?

10. Who scored a First Division hat-trick against Queen's Park Rangers on the opening day of the 1986/87 Football League season, his first ever game in the First Division?

41 *Football Awards*

1. Who, in 1948, became the first winner of the Football Writers' Association Footballer of the Year award?

2. Who, in 1987, was voted Footballer of the Year by both the Football Writers and his fellow professionals?

3. Who was the first goalkeeper to win the Footballer of the Year award?

4. Who is the only footballer to have won the European Player of the Year award three years in succession?

5. Who was the second British player to become European Footballer of the Year, Stanley Matthews having won the inaugural award in 1956?

6. Who is the only British footballer to have retained the European Footballer of the Year award?

7. Who was the Cameroon goalkeeper, a star in the 1982 World Cup finals, who was voted African Footballer of the Year in both 1979 and 1982?

8. Which British footballer won the Golden Boot award as Europe's highest League goalscorer in 1983/84?

9. Which two British footballers were in a three-way tie for third place behind Gerd Muller in the 1972 Golden Boot award, having scored thirty-three League goals apiece?

10. Who was the Chilean international who was voted South American Player of the Year three years in succession between 1974 and 1976?

42 *Playing Days*

Which current managers* were involved in the following transfer deals during their playing careers?

1. December 1970, Gillingham to Bournemouth and Boscombe Athletic, £9,000.

2. January 1973, Tottenham Hotspur to Middlesbrough, £30,000.

3. September 1974, Everton to Sheffield Wednesday, £70,000.

4. November 1974, Manchester United to Portsmouth, player exchange deal also involving Ron Davies.

5. December 1975, West Ham United to Wolverhampton Wanderers, £30,000.

6. August 1979, Coventry City to Tottenham Hotspur, £275,000.

7. August 1977, Birmingham City to Stoke City, £40,000.

8. December 1977, Manchester City to Bristol City, £90,000.

9. September 1978, Tottenham Hotspur to Derby County, £150,000.

10. March 1959, Heart of Midlothian to Tottenham Hotspur, £35,000.

* Correct as at July 1988.

43 *Football League—Mixed Bag*

1. Who has recently retired as general secretary of the Football Association?

2. For which club did this former general secretary play eight League matches as a centre-half in 1950?

3. Who made his League début for Nottingham Forest against Arsenal in September 1978 at sixteen years of age – though this initial promise was rather slow to fulfil itself, as he was only to play forty-seven first-team games in his first eight seasons with the club?

4. Who, at eighteen years of age, was appointed captain of Chelsea in the 1974/75 season?

5. Which player made his League début in 1964 at the age of twenty-nine, and within five years had captained his club to both the League championship and victory in the FA Cup Final?

6. Which midfield trio played in all forty-two games for the League champions, Aston Villa, in 1980/81?

7. Which club side retained the same goalkeeper, two full-backs and three half-backs for all forty-two League games in 1952/53, when winning promotion from the Second Division?

8. Which was the first team after the Second World War to win the League championship in successive seasons?

9. Which was the last club to be promoted from the Fourth Division in its first season in the Football League?

10. Which one of the original twelve members of the Football League has relinquished its League status?

44 *The 1986 Mexico World Cup Finals*

1. Who appeared as a substitute for England fifteen minutes from the end of the quarter-final match against Argentina, showing exceptional skill to create two clear scoring opportunities?

2. Disregarding subsequent transfers, who was the only Liverpool player involved in the 1986 tournament?

3. Which country eliminated Italy, the defending champions, with a 2–0 victory in the second round of the 1986 tournament?

4. Who was the Northern Ireland captain who was honoured with an MBE during the 1986 tournament?

5. Which captain was left out of the team for his country's final group match against Uruguay, after failing to exert his normal influence in the previous two games?

6. Who captained England for three and a half matches out of five in the 1986 tournament?

7. Which country, in its first World Cup tournament, was eliminated without scoring a goal?

8. Who was the only player to score in both the semi-final and final of the tournament?

9. Who scored the final goal in the competition, to seal Argentina's 3–2 victory over West Germany?

10. Who was the manager of Argentina in the tournament?

45 The European Cup Winners' Cup – Clubs

1. Which British club was beaten on the 'away goals' rule in the second round of the 1986/87 tournament, by Real Zaragoza?

2. Which club, managed by Johan Cruyff, won the trophy for the first time in 1987?

3. Which British club conceded only two goals in the competition, to Bayern Munich and Rapid Vienna, when winning it in 1984/85?

4. Which club overturned a 3–0 defeat at Parkhead with a 1–0 victory at Old Trafford, after Celtic had been ordered to replay their second-round home leg in 1985 at least 100 miles from Glasgow, following serious crowd disturbances in the first match?

5. Which British club held Manchester City, the holders, to a draw in the first round of the 1970/71 competition, losing only on the 'away goals' rule?

6. Which British club was knocked out by Honved in the first round in 1970/71, losing the first penalty shoot-out to decide the outcome of a tie in European competition?

7. Which British club lifted the trophy in 1972, but was banned from the competition for the following season because of the behaviour of its supporters?

8. Which Czechoslovakian club beat Barcelona in the 1969 final, to become the first team from behind the Iron Curtain to win the trophy?

9. Who became the first British winners of a European club competition, when they won the Cup Winners' Cup in 1962/63?

10. Which club won the inaugural European Cup Winners' Cup, beating Glasgow Rangers in 1960/61 – the only occasion that the final has been played over two legs, on a home-and-away basis?

46 Mixed Bag

1. Which Englishman was dismissed as manager of the Portuguese club, Belenenses, in November 1985, after having guided them to promotion from the Second Division only the previous season?

2. Who, in December 1985, played his first game for Luton Town since leaving the club in April 1976 to join Everton?

3. Which Third Division club beat the FA Cup holders, Manchester United, in the third round of the 1983/84 competition?

4. Which player, who ended his ten-year Football League career playing for Tranmere Rovers in 1968/69, has been manager of non-league Telford United during their recent annual FA Cup giant-killing performances?

5. Who was dismissed in January 1984, after six and a half years as manager of Reading, at a time when the club was lying in third place in the Fourth Division?

6. Which club defeated promoted Newcastle United in April 1984, so ending a record run of thirty-one League matches without a victory, stretching back over six months to October 1983, when they had defeated Oldham Athletic?

7. Which former West Bromwich Albion full-back became Assistant Secretary of the Professional Footballers' Association in May 1984, having been forced to retire as a player through injury?

8. Who was the amateur who was capped in 1936 for England against Belgium, and also played in that year's Olympic Games tournament?

9. Who was forced to retire from the game in 1984 with a hip injury at the age of twenty-six, having four years earlier been the subject of a £1 million transfer?

10. Who was suspended from football throughout the world in October 1984, for failure to pay a £250 fine imposed by the Football Association for remarks he made to a referee after a Football League Second Division match in February 1984, when he was manager of Middlesbrough?

47 England Players

1. Which club provided six players – in addition to another who had recently been transferred – for the England team that played a goalless draw with Switzerland at Wembley in September 1977?

2. Which club provided seven players for England's game against Italy at Highbury in November 1934?

3. Who, in a European Nations Cup match against Yugoslavia in Florence in June 1968, became the first England player to be sent off in an international?

4. Who was the South African-born winger who represented England on three occasions between November 1955 and April 1956?

5. Who was the winger from recently relegated Sheffield United who scored two goals on his England début, in a 4–2 win over Brazil at Wembley in May 1956, the first match between the two countries?

6. Who netted England's only goal in their 4–1 defeat by Peru in Lima in May 1959, to maintain his record of scoring on his début for every team in which he played?

7. Which Huddersfield Town winger scored twice for England on his début against Northern Ireland in October 1962, but had to wait until March 1969, when he was a Leeds player, for his second and last international appearance, when he scored again in a 5–0 win over France?

8. When Ray Wilson won his sixty-third and last cap, in the 2–0 European Nations Cup win over the USSR in Rome in June 1968, who was his Everton colleague and full-back partner who won the first of his eleven caps in the same game?

9. Which Arsenal defender won his only England cap in the 1–1 draw with Yugoslavia at Wembley in October 1972?

10. Who was the twenty-year-old who became the first player born after the 1966 World Cup to play for England in a full international match when he made his début against Spain in Madrid in February 1987?

48 *Football League—Mixed Bag*

1. Which two brothers scored the goals in a 1–1 draw between Wolverhampton Wanderers and Newcastle United at Molineux, in Division I, in February 1975?

2. Who were the father and son who played for Stockport County against Hartlepool United in a Third Division North game in May 1951?

3. Which is the only club to have played continuously in the First Division since the end of the First World War?

4. Which club, a founder member of the Football League in 1888, has spent only four seasons outside the First Division?

5. Who was given a free transfer by Manchester United at the end of the 1972/73 season, after scoring 171 goals in 309 League games for the club, signed for neighbours Manchester City and, in the last League match of his career in May 1974 scored the only goal of the derby game at Old Trafford, which effectively relegated United?

6. Who managed Charlton Athletic for twenty-three years up to 1956, leading them from the Third Division South to the First Division in successive seasons, and winning the FA Cup in 1947?

7. Which member of Tottenham Hotspur's 'double'-winning team in 1960/61 was player-manager of First Division Queen's Park Rangers in 1968/69?

8. Which club played continuously in the First Division from 1888 to 1958?

9. Which club was undefeated in its first twenty-nine Division I League matches in the 1973/74 season?

10. Which club won the championship in 1959/60, although it never led the Division I table before the final match of the season?

49 World Cup Captains

1. Which English-born player captained Scotland in the 1978 World Cup tournament?

2. Who was the captain of Brazil in both the 1982 and 1986 World Cup tournaments?

3. Who captained Northern Ireland in the 1982 tournament?

4. Who captained England in three World Cups?

5. Who was the forty-year-old who led his country to victory in a World Cup?

6. Who was the captain, playing in his 100th international, who missed a penalty against the host nation, Argentina, in the 1978 tournament?

7. Who captained Wales in 1958, the only time that the principality has qualified to play in the World Cup finals?

8. Who was the captain of West Germany in both the 1966 and 1970 tournaments?

9. Who captained Italy in the 1938 World Cup after playing in the 1934 tournament, the only team captain with two World Cup winner's medals?

10. Which Uruguayan defender became the first World Cup winning captain in 1930?

50 *Scots in the Football League*

1. Which Edinburgh-born full-back, between 1961 and 1976, played a club record 560 League games for Aston Villa?

2. Who, in 1965, became the first Scottish-born footballer to win the Football Writers' Association Footballer of the Year award?

3. Who was the legendary Scottish centre-forward who scored 133 goals for Newcastle United in 155 matches between 1925 and 1930?

4. Who was the tiny Scottish inside forward, with the long baggy pants, who was the linchpin of the famous Arsenal side of the 1930s?

5. Which South African-born full-back played 495 League games for Charlton Athletic between 1951 and 1965, as well as winning nineteen caps for Scotland?

6. Which member of Liverpool's 1965 F A Cup winning team had previously won a Scottish Cup winner's medal with Rangers?

7. Who captained an F A Cup winning team at Wembley seven years after leading his previous club to victory in the Scottish F A Cup?

8. Who made 304 League appearances for Manchester United after signing from Celtic in February 1963?

9. Who has played more than 300 League games and scored more than 100 goals for his only English League club, having previously achieved the same feat in Scotland?

10. Who scored twenty-six League goals for West Ham United in 1985/86, his first season in the Football League after transferring from St Mirren?

51 *The FA Cup – Players*

1. Who, in 1985, played in his fifth FA Cup final in only eight seasons?

2. Who was the seventeen-year-old who gained an FA Cup winner's medal in 1980, when he became the youngest player to appear in an FA Cup final?

3. Who was the eighteen-year-old who scored the second goal in the 1983 FA Cup final replay, the youngest player to score in a final?

4. Who, in 1964 became the youngest player to score in an FA Cup final when, as an eighteen-year-old, he scored West Ham United's opening goal against Preston North End?

5. Which seventeen-year-old appeared for Preston North End in the 1964 final, breaking the record for the youngest ever FA Cup finalist previously set by Arsenal's Cliff Bastin in 1930, and subsequently broken again in 1980?

6. Who was the Manchester United substitute who replaced an out-of-form Gordon Hill in both the 1976 and 1977 FA Cup finals?

7. Who became the first substitute to score in an FA Cup final when he was credited with Arsenal's equalizing goal against Liverpool in 1971?

8. Who became the first substitute to play in an FA Cup final when, in 1968, he replaced John Kaye at the beginning of extra time, in West Bromwich Albion's 1–0 victory over Everton?

9. Who was credited with scoring for both sides in the 1987 FA Cup final?

10. Who, in 1946, became the first player to score for both sides in an FA Cup final at Wembley when, in the space of a minute, he conceded an own goal to give Derby County the lead, and then equalized for Charlton Athletic?

52 *The European Cup – Mixed Bag*

1. Who was the Steaua Bucharest goalkeeper who saved all four penalties against him in the 1986 European Cup Final shoot-out?

2. Who came on as substitute for Aston Villa after just eight minutes of the 1982 final, and played superbly in only his second senior match?

3. Which club, in the first round in 1967/68, became the first to beat Celtic, the holders, at Parkhead in the European Cup, and went on to knock them out of the competition?

4. Which club, in 1965/66, became the first Irish League representatives to win a European Cup tie, with an 8–6 aggregate victory over Lyn Oslo, only to withdraw from the competition after a 9–0 thrashing by Anderlecht in the first leg of the second round?

5. Which British club, competing in its first European Cup, reached the semi-final without conceding a goal?

6. Who won six European Cup winner's medals, playing in eight finals?

7. Who played against Real Madrid in the first European Cup Final, and for them in the next three finals?

8. Who was the manager of Panathinaikos, the Greek club which reached the 1971 final?

9. Who was the manager of Aston Villa when the club won the 1981/82 competition?

10. Who scored both AC Milan's goals in the 1963 final against Benfica at Wembley, and played for Juventus against Ajax in the 1973 final?

53 *Football League Managers*

1. Who managed Huddersfield Town to the Second Division championship in 1969/70, and Bolton Wanderers to the same achievement in 1977/78?

2. Who was the manager of Queen's Park Rangers, Division II champions in 1982/83, and also of Crystal Palace, Division II winners in 1978/79?

3. Who is the only manager to have led the same club to the championships of the Third, Second and First Divisions of the Football League?

4. Who was the Irishman who managed Newport County in 1938/39, Cardiff City in 1946/47 and Swansea Town in 1948/49, each of the three Welsh clubs comfortably winning the Third Division South championship in those seasons?

5. Which current First Division manager has guided two different clubs to the Football League championship?

6. Who is the only manager to have led two different clubs to more than one Football League championship each?

7. Who retired in 1986, with the unique record of managing five different Football League clubs on two separate occasions?

8. Which former Manchester United player succeeded Matt Busby in 1970 as the club's manager?

9. Which manager led Doncaster Rovers to the Division IV championship in 1968/69 and Grimsby Town to the same achievement in 1971/72?

10. Which First Division manager has held his current post since August 1974?

54 *National Club Champions Worldwide*

1. Which club achieved a rare double in 1986/87 by winning both the Italian cup and the league championship?

2. Which club retained the Belgian soccer championship in 1986 after a two-leg play-off with RFC Bruges?

3. Which club won the Soviet league title in 1986 by a single point, having been awarded one extra point from a drawn match for supplying so many players to the World Cup squad?

4. Which club won the Northern Ireland league championship in 1987 for the sixth year in succession, and for the ninth time in ten years?

5. Who were the 1985 French league champions who lost 9–0 to Monaco in January 1986?

6. Which club won the Republic of Ireland league championship for the third successive year in 1986?

7. Which club won the first World Club Championship in 1960 with a 5–1 aggregate victory over Penarol of Uruguay?

8. Which Argentine club beat Manchester United for the 1968 World Club Championship by a one-goal margin?

9. Which Brazilian club beat Liverpool 3–0 in December 1981 in the National Stadium, Tokyo, thereby keeping the World Club Championship in South American hands?

10. Which is the only European team to have retained the World Club Championship – and, in fact, the only club from the northern hemisphere to have won the title more than once?

55 *World Cup Goalscorers*

1. Who was the leading goalscorer in the 1986 tournament?

2. Who failed to score in his first four matches in the 1982 tournament, but finished as the leading goalscorer?

3. Who scored three goals for Hungary in a 10–1 victory over El Salvador in the 1982 tournament after coming on to the field as a substitute?

4. Who scored a total of five goals in the 1978 tournament, including four penalties?

5. Who scored seven times in seven matches to finish as the leading scorer in the 1974 tournament?

6. Who shares with Pele the distinction of scoring in all four World Cup tournaments between 1958 and 1970?

7. Who scored five goals for Peru in the 1970 World Cup and, on his country's next appearance in the tournament in 1978, scored twice against Scotland in the opening match?

8. Who was the Frenchman who set an individual scoring record for a single World Cup with thirteen goals in the 1958 tournament?

9. Who scored eleven goals in the 1954 tournament, including four in one match against West Germany, the eventual champions?

10. Who scored four goals for Poland against Brazil in 1938, yet his team still lost 6–5 after extra time, and was eliminated after playing just one game in their first appearance in a World Cup tournament?

56 *Football League—Mixed Bag*

1. Which London-based winger won promotion from Division III with Queen's Park Rangers in 1966/67, from Division II with Crystal Palace in 1968/69 and from Division III with Orient in 1969/70?

2. Which south coast club, runners-up in the Third Division South in six successive seasons from 1921/22 to 1926/27, was third in 1928/29 before eventually gaining promotion in 1929/30?

3. Which club lost only three League games in 1978/79 but still finished eight points behind Liverpool in the championship?

4. Which was the only club, prior to the introduction of three points for a win, to win the First Division title with more points to its credit than goals scored?

5. Which club, finishing fifth in Division I in 1957/58, scored 104 goals and conceded 100, the only occasion that a League tally has reached three figures in both 'for' and 'against' columns?

6. Which club, in its first fourteen years in the Football League, won an FA Cup Final at Wembley, played eight seasons in the First Division, and had to apply for re-election to the Third Division South?

7. Which club scored a record 128 First Division goals in 1930/31, but finished the season seven points behind Arsenal in the championship?

8. Which club was relegated from the First Division in 1963/64 after conceding 121 goals, the highest total since Blackpool conceded 125 in 1930/31?

9. Which club, no longer a member of the Football League, won the Division IV championship in 1972/73 – a season made memorable because all four divisions were headed by clubs from Lancashire?

10. Which club, in spite of being relegated in 1973/74, supplied that season's leading Division I goalscorer?

57 *The Inter-Cities Fairs Cup/European Fairs Cup/UEFA Cup – Players*

1. Which British player scored a hat-trick of penalties in his club's 5–1 victory over Aris Salonika of Greece, in their first-round first leg tie in the 1980/81 UEFA Cup?

2. Which player twice scored four goals for Ipswich in UEFA Cup ties, first in the 4–0 home win over Lazio in 1973/74, and then four years later in the 5–0 home victory over Landskrona?

3. Charlie George and Leighton James both scored three goals in Derby County's 12–0 UEFA Cup first-leg victory over Finn Harps in September 1976, but who surpassed them both by scoring five times in the match?

4. Who scored three hat-tricks for Queen's Park Rangers in the 1976/77 UEFA Cup competition, one in each leg of the first-round tie with Brann Bergen and another in the second-round home leg against Slovan Bratislava?

5. Who scored a hat-trick for Borussia Moenchengladbach in the 1975 UEFA Cup Final against Twenty Enschede, taking his total to eleven goals in that season's competition?

6. Who, in his first European match, scored a hat-trick for Wolverhampton Wanderers against Academica Coimbra in the first round of the 1971/72 UEFA Cup?

7. Which current English Football League player scored for AZ 67 Alkmaar against Ipswich Town in the 1981 UEFA Cup Final?

8. Who was the Newcastle United captain and centre-back who scored three goals over the two legs of the 1969 European Fairs Cup Final?

9. Who, in the 1965/66 Inter-cities Fairs Cup, was the thirty-nine-year-old centre-forward for Espanol who helped his club to the quarter-finals, where they lost to their near neighbours and the eventual competition winners, Barcelona?

10. Which former Hungarian World Cup star scored Barcelona's three goals in the 1962 Inter-Cities Fairs Cup Final?

58 Eire Internationals

1. Who was the Glasgow-born midfield player who, in March 1986, made his international début for Eire against Wales in Dublin?

2. Who was left out of the Republic of Ireland team against Uruguay in April 1986, for the first time since making his début more than ten years earlier?

3. Who made his début for Eire against China in 1984, in the same week as his first match for Liverpool?

4. Who were the two brothers who formed Eire's central defence partnership in four internationals in 1980 and 1981?

5. Which famous Irish footballer won twenty-nine caps between 1938 and 1953, and was the only player to represent the Republic both before and after the Second World War?

6. Which famous midfield player of the 1960s and 1970s won sixty caps for Eire, many as captain, in a twenty-year career, before later serving his country as manager?

7. Which Everton wing-half, playing as an inside-forward, scored Eire's second goal in their 2–0 win over England at Goodison Park in September 1949?

8. Who won the first and last of his fifty-one caps for Eire as a Shamrock Rovers player, but spent most of his eleven-year international career, between 1969 and 1980, in the Football League, with Chelsea, Crystal Palace and West Bromwich Albion?

9. Who was the Eire inside-forward who died in the Munich air crash at the age of twenty-two?

10. Who won nine caps for Eire as a player with West Ham United and Preston North End during the 1950s, and in the early 1970s managed Manchester United?

59 Football League Divisions III and IV

1. Which club was the first to obtain 100 points in a League season, when it won the Fourth Division championship in the 1983/84 season?

2. Which Third Division side won its first thirteen League matches in 1985/86 and went on to gain promotion as champions?

3. Which club scored more than 100 League goals in winning the championship of Division IV in 1986/87?

4. Which club won its final League match in the 1986/87 season to avoid dropping out of the Football League, after a membership of ninety-nine years, during which it has twice won the First Division championship, and as recently as 1981/82 gained promotion to the First Division?

5. Which team joined the Football League for the first time in the season 1987/88?

6. Which Third Division team, in successive home League games, scored eight goals and then a club record ten, at the start of the 1987/88 season?

7. Which club was either promoted from or relegated to the Fourth Division for five successive seasons from 1978/79 to 1982/83, before ending the sequence by winning promotion to the Second Division in 1983/84?

8. Which club, an original member of the Football League, had to apply for re-election when finishing ninety-first out of ninety-two in the season 1985/86, a sad decline after eighty-two successive years in the top two divisions prior to 1970?

9. Which club finished ninety-second in the Football League in the 1984/85 and 1985/86 seasons, and only survived in the Fourth Division in 1986/87 by virtue of a superior goal-difference?

10. Which club won the Fourth Division championship in 1975/76 with a record seventy-four points, winning thirty-two of forty-six matches played and losing only four?

60 *Mixed Bag*

1. Who replaced Peter Shilton in goal for the second half of the Centenary Match between the Football League and the Rest of the World in August 1987?

2. Which seventeen-year-old, yet to make his first-team début for the Merseysiders, signed for Liverpool from Oldham Athletic for £250,000 in January 1985, and was immediately loaned back for the remainder of the season?

3. Who was the seventeen-year-old who was transferred to Manchester City from Crystal Palace for £275,000 in July 1979, though he had never played a first-team game for the Londoners?

4. Who was the leading goalscorer in the Spanish first division in 1984/85, who was transferred from Athletico to Real Madrid before the start of the following season?

5. Who, after managing Preston North End to the 1954 FA Cup Final, had a successful thirteen-year period as manager of Glasgow Rangers?

6. Who, in 1985, became the ninth post-war player to appear in both Scottish and English FA Cup winning teams?

7. Which club had its worst ever start to a Football League season in 1985/86, losing the first five matches without scoring a single goal?

8. Who scored a record thirteen goals in one match, when Arbroath beat Bon Accord 36–0 in the first round of the Scottish Cup in September 1885?

9. Which First Division club drew its opening game of the 1985/86 season, against Oxford United, and then suffered nine League defeats in a row, hastening its manager's resignation?

10. Who was the twenty-nine-year-old club captain who accepted the position of manager of Doncaster Rovers in October 1985, following Billy Bremner's move to Leeds United?

61 *The FA Cup – Giant-killers*

1. Which Third Division side, though in danger of relegation to Division IV, reached the semi-final of the 1983/84 competition, before losing 1–0 to Watford at Villa Park?

2. Which Third Division side scored from a last-minute penalty to beat Arsenal in the fourth round in 1984/85, drawing with Liverpool in the next round before crashing out 7–0 in the Anfield replay?

3. Which Third Division side reached the fifth round in 1986/87, having enjoyed away wins against First Division Charlton Athletic and Second Division Birmingham City, but then lost 1–0, by an own goal, to Watford in a second replay?

4. Which Fourth Division side caused a sensation in 1970/71 by beating the Cup favourites, Leeds United, in the fifth round before going down 5–0 at Everton in the quarter-final?

5. Which lowly placed Second Division club beat the First Division champions elect, Liverpool, 2–1 at Anfield in a 1963/64 quarter-final?

6. Which modest Third Division outfit beat West Ham United 3–0 in the 1968/69 fifth round, reaching the quarter-final for the only time in their history, and lost 1–0 at home to the eventual finalists, Leicester City?

7. Which famous cup-fighting side, then in the Third Division North, forced the eventual winners, Newcastle United, to a semi-final replay in 1954/55?

8. Which Third Division North side created a major shock in the 1953/54 competition by defeating the holders, Blackpool, in the fifth round and progressing to the semi-final, where they narrowly lost to West Bromwich Albion, the eventual winners?

9. Which Third Division side took First Division Luton Town to a semi-final replay in 1959?

10. Which club from the Third Division South beat the First Division champions elect, Manchester City, in the 1936/37 quarter-final, losing 2–1 to the eventual winners, Sunderland, in the semi-final?

62 *England in the Final Stages of the World Cup*

1. Who was the captain of the England squad in the 1982 World Cup who, because of injury, made his only appearance as a late second-half substitute against Spain in the team's final match of the tournament?

2. Which three players shared England's six goals in the 1982 tournament?

3. Who, just minutes after replacing Francis Lee, almost equalized for England against Brazil in the 1970 tournament?

4. Who netted both of England's goals in the 1966 semi-final against Portugal – the last time he was to score in World Cup football?

5. Which England captain made his final international appearance in the 1962 quarter-final match against Brazil?

6. Who scored England's first two goals in the 1962 tournament, both from the penalty spot?

7. Who became the first player to score for England in two World Cups, scoring just one goal in both the 1954 and 1958 tournaments, against Uruguay and USSR respectively?

8. In which year did England become the first UK nation to play in a World Cup tournament?

9. Which country did England beat by two goals to nil in their first ever World Cup tournament match?

10. Which country caused a sensation when handing England their first defeat in World Cup finals?

63 *Football League Clubs – Mixed Bag*

1. Which team were First Division runners-up five times in eight seasons between 1964 and 1972?

2. Which was the only club to win the Second Division championship three times in the 1950s?

3. Which club won its only First Division championship after the Second World War, and achieved the feat with only fifty-two points, equalling the lowest winning total since the division was extended to twenty-two teams in 1919/20, a record previously shared by Sheffield Wednesday (1928/29) and Arsenal (1937/38)?

4. Which club, in 1962/63, in its first season in the Fourth Division, became the first to have played against all ninety-one of its Football League contemporaries in the League itself?

5. Which club was relegated at the end of the 1925/26 season, despite scoring eighty-nine goals in the First Division, a total only exceeded by four other clubs?

6. Which club finished bottom of the First Division in 1928/29, despite conceding only fifty-nine goals, two fewer than any of the twenty-one clubs above them in the table?

7. Which is the only club to have scored more than 100 First Division goals in each of four consecutive seasons?

8. Which club, in 1958/59, became the first champions of the Fourth Division?

9. Which club won promotion from the Fourth Division in 1977/78, finished sixth in the First Division in 1981/82, after briefly heading the table, and returned to the Fourth Division at the end of 1985/86?

10. Which club won the Second Division championship in 1969/70, was relegated from the top division in 1971/72, dropped into the Third for the first time in its history a year later, and then went down still further into the Fourth Division at the end of the 1974/75 season?

64 Record Transfers

1. Which foreign player, in October 1978, became Birmingham's City's record signing at £259,000, a fee surpassed the following year when the club purchased Colin Todd from Everton?

2. Prior to buying Andy Gray for a reputed £1,469,000 in September 1979, Wolverhampton Wanderers' record signature had been a comparatively modest £150,000, when they bought which player from Hull City in May 1978?

3. Which player did Charlton Athletic sign from Tampa Bay Rowdies in August 1979 for £135,000, the fee being a new record for the Londoners, and their first purchase in excess of £100,000?

4. Stoke City bought Alan Hudson from Chelsea for a club record £240,000 in January 1974, but to which club did they sell him in December 1976, the £225,000 transaction another record for the Potteries club?

5. Which player, destined to play in only thirty-nine matches for the club before injury forced his premature retirement, did Manchester United sign for £200,000 in March 1972, a club record that lasted until January 1978, when Joe Jordan came from Leeds United for £350,000?

6. Whom did Norwich City sign from Rochdale for a record £40,000 in October 1971 and sell to Coventry City for a further record £150,000 two years later?

7. Before they signed Bob Latchford from Birmingham City in February 1974, the first £300,000 transfer between British clubs, Everton's record signing had been when they paid £180,000 to Aberdeen, for which Scottish international striker?

8. Which player, originally a foreign import, was transferred from Sheffield United to Leeds United in May 1980 for £400,000, a record for both clubs?

9. Which Welsh international was transferred from Arsenal to Birmingham City for £140,000 in October 1972, both a record sale for the Londoners and a record purchase for the Midland side?

10. When Martin Peters joined Tottenham Hotspur from West Ham United in March 1970 as the first £200,000 player in British soccer, who moved in the opposite direction at a valuation of £80,000?

65 *The European Cup – Goalscorers*

1. Who scored the only goal of the ill-fated 1985 final between Juventus and Liverpool, in the Heysel Stadium, Brussels?

2. Who scored the only goal for SV Hamburg in their 1983 final victory over Juventus?

3. Who scored the only goal of the 1980 final, enabling the holders, Nottingham Forest, to retain the trophy?

4. Who scored the winning goal for Celtic in the 1967 final?

5. Which British player scored seven goals in a European Cup tie against Floriana of Malta?

6. Who was the first British footballer to be leading goalscorer in the European Cup, scoring nine goals in the competition in 1956/57?

7. Who was the twenty-two-year-old, playing in only his second first-class match, who scored Nottingham Forest's opening goal against Liverpool in their 1978/79 tie?

8. Who scored four goals in his first European Cup Final and three in his second?

9. Who is the only striker to have been leading goalscorer in the European Cup for two successive seasons?

10. Who has scored a record forty-nine goals in the European Cup?

66 *Scotland Internationals*

1. Who played against Yugoslavia in November 1956 to become the first player to obtain fifty caps for Scotland, finishing with fifty-three in an international career extending from November 1946 to May 1957?

2. Who appeared as a second-half substitute for Gordon Strachan in the World Cup qualifying match with Wales, in Cardiff in September 1985, and scored the equalizing goal from the penalty spot, virtually ensuring that Scotland would qualify for Mexico?

3. Who scored Scotland's equalizer against England in the 1–1 draw at Hampden Park in May 1984, the final goal for his country in a home international championship match?

4. Who won his fiftieth and final cap for Scotland in the 1982 World Cup match with Brazil?

5. Who was capped at schoolboy, youth, amateur and under-23 level before making the first of his twenty-one senior appearances for Scotland, as a substitute against Austria in November 1969?

6. Who scored four goals for Scotland against Northern Ireland on 7 November 1962, and four against Norway on 7 November 1963?

7. Which Rangers centre-half was regularly selected for Scotland between 1966 and 1971 in preference to Celtic's Billy McNeill?

8. For which club was Alan Rough playing when he made his fifty-third appearance for Scotland in September 1985, having won all his previous caps as a Partick Thistle player?

9. Who made his début for Scotland in the summer of 1979, after signing for Liverpool, but failed to win a place in the Merseyside team and was transferred back to his homeland in March 1980?

10. Which versatile defender and midfield player's international career ended at its peak after the 1974 World Cup, when he was sidelined for many months by a serious eye problem, after which he never recovered his earlier form?

67 World Cup Managers

1. Who was the manager of Italy in 1986 for the third successive World Cup?

2. Who served as England's manager through four World Cups between 1950 and 1962?

3. Who was the chain-smoking manager of Argentina in 1978 when they won the World Cup for the first time?

4. Who managed West Germany to second, third and first place respectively in successive tournaments between 1966 and 1974?

5. Who resigned as Scotland's team manager during the 1954 World Cup tournament?

6. Who played for his native Uruguay in the 1954 World Cup, then transferred his allegiance to play for Spain in 1962, and was the Spanish team manager for the 1982 tournament?

7. Who was the extrovert manager of Scotland in the 1978 tournament?

8. Who was the famous former international who managed the Northern Ireland team in the 1958 World Cup?

9. Who was the Englishman who managed Sweden in both the 1950 and 1958 World Cups?

10. Who was the manager of the Italian teams which won the World Cup both in 1934 and 1938?

68 Football League – One-club Players

1. Who was the England captain who played 568 games for Blackpool between 1954 and 1970?

2. Who scored 255 goals in 452 appearances for Bolton Wanderers between 1946 and 1960?

3. Who played a record 595 games for Tranmere Rovers between 1946 and 1960, including a League record 401 consecutive appearances?

4. Who, between 1960 and 1980, played a League record 770 games for Swindon Town?

5. Who set a record of 385 League appearances for Oxford United between 1962 and 1971, before switching to a career in football management?

6. Which player made 433 League appearances for Preston North End between 1946 and 1960, scoring 187 goals?

7. Which England stalwart played 764 League games for Portsmouth between 1946 and 1964?

8. Who scored 145 goals in 594 League games for Fulham between 1952 and 1969?

9. Which Scottish international footballer scored 216 goals for Liverpool in 492 League games between 1946 and 1960?

10. Who was the Scottish-born centre-half who made 614 League appearances for Nottingham Forest between 1951 and 1970?

69 *England Players*

1. Who became England's first ever substitute in a full international, replacing Jackie Milburn in the 4–1 win over Belgium in Brussels in May 1950?

2. Who were the Sheffield-born cousins who played together in four matches for England between November 1952 and June 1953, both making their last appearance in a 6–3 win over the USA in New York?

3. Which Sunderland wing-half won four England caps between November 1949 and November 1950, each on different English League grounds, and in June 1951 gained the first of twenty-three England cricket caps?

4. Which player, later to win more fame as a manager, made his only England appearance in May 1951, and scored the first goal in a 5–2 victory over Portugal?

5. Which Arsenal winger won his only England cap against Austria in November 1951, and seven years later scored a century on his England cricket début?

6. Which West Bromwich Albion forward scored two of England's six goals against Switzerland at Highbury in December 1948, his only international?

7. Who was the Fulham centre-forward, and later club manager, who won the first of his two caps against Hungary in Budapest in May 1954, when England suffered a humiliating 7–1 defeat?

8. Which two players formed an England full-back partnership for seventeen consecutive games between October 1955 and May 1957, both later dying at the age of twenty-nine, in separate but equally tragic circumstances?

9. Who began his England career as a left full-back in 1959 but, after four games, switched to right-back for his last thirty-nine international appearances?

10. Who was the goalkeeper from Third Division Coventry City who played five games for England during 1956?

70 *The Football League Cup/Milk Cup/Littlewoods Cup*

1. Who scored a record twelve goals in the Littlewoods Cup during the 1986/87 season?

2. Which club won the 1987 Littlewoods Cup final, ending, after 144 matches, Liverpool's record of avoiding defeat when Ian Rush had scored?

3. Which club's first ever Wembley final brought a 3–0 victory over Queen's Park Rangers in the 1986 Milk Cup?

4. Which two teams contested the 1985 Milk Cup final and were then both relegated from the First Division at the end of the season?

5. Which club won the League Cup/Milk Cup four times in succession between 1981 and 1984?

6. Which manager led three different clubs to League Cup finals in successive seasons?

7. Which was the first club to play in three consecutive League Cup finals?

8. Which is the only Fourth Division club to have played in a League Cup final?

9. Which teams, in 1963, contested the first League Cup final between Division I clubs?

10. Which club, in 1967, won the first League Cup final to be played at Wembley, and ended the season as runaway champions of the Third Division?

71 Overseas Players in the Football League

1. Who scored both goals in the 1972 Olympic Final and later played thirty-eight League games for Manchester City?

2. Who, when transferred from River Plate to Sheffield United in August 1978, became the third Argentinian to join the Football League?

3. By what name is Francisco Ernandi Lima da Silva, the first Brazilian to play in the Football League, better known?

4. Who was the Yugoslavian international goalkeeper who signed for Chelsea from Partizan Belgrade, making more than 100 League appearances for the Londoners between 1979 and 1981?

5. Which Danish international forward, signed from Barcelona in October 1982, had a short stay with Charlton Athletic, who needed to part with a club record transfer payment of £324,000 to secure his services?

6. Which two members of Liverpool's League and Cup Double winning side in 1985/86 were born in Durban and Johannesburg respectively?

7. Who is the current Nigerian international forward who has played League Football with Orient, Notts County and Tottenham Hotspur?

8. Who was the Yugoslavian international defender who played 144 League matches for Southampton between November 1978 and November 1982, and in March 1979 became the first overseas player to appear in a League Cup Final at Wembley?

9. Who was the Yugoslavian international midfield player whose 100 League games for Luton Town between August 1980 and May 1984 included forty-six appearances as substitute?

10. Which overseas player was, in 1981, voted Footballer of the Year by the Football Writers' Association?

72 Brazil in the World Cup

1. Who scored five goals for Brazil during the 1986 tournament?

2. Who scored a hat-trick against Brazil in the 1982 tournament?

3. Who was the Brazilian captain who scored the final goal in their victory over Italy to win the 1970 World Cup?

4. Who gained World Cup winner's medals for Brazil as a player in 1958 and 1962, and as the manager in 1970?

5. Who played for Brazil in the 1954, 1958 and 1962 tournaments, and in 1970 managed the Peruvian team which lost to Brazil in the quarter-final?

6. Who scored in all six of Brazil's matches during the 1970 tournament?

7. Who was allowed by FIFA to play for Brazil in the 1962 World Cup Final against Czechoslovakia, despite being sent off in the semi-final against Chile?

8. Who remains the only player to have scored in consecutive World Cup Finals, netting for Brazil in both 1958 and 1962?

9. Who scored his first World Cup goal for Brazil in a 1–0 victory over Wales in the 1958 quarter-final?

10. Which country, having beaten Brazil in the quarter-final in 1954, became the next team to beat them again in the competition, with a 3–1 victory at Goodison Park in 1966?

73 *The European Cup Winners' Cup – Mixed Bag*

1. Which British club was undefeated throughout the competition and yet didn't win the trophy?

2. Which team set a European club record with a 16–1 home victory over Apoel Nicosia in the second round of the 1963/64 competition?

3. Which British club won a first-round Cup Winners' Cup tie by an aggregate score of 21–0?

4. Which was the first club to lose in two Cup Winners' Cup Finals?

5. Which British team beat Barcelona 3–0 in the 1983/84 quarter-final, when they were two goals down from the first leg – the first time that the Catalan side had surrendered a two-goal lead in a European tie?

6. Which is the only club to have scored five goals in a Cup Winners' Cup Final?

7. Which was the first English team to play in the competition, going out 3–1 on aggregate to Rangers in the 1961 semi-final?

8. Which team, in 1972, became the first Soviet club to compete in the final of a European club competition, when they played Rangers in the Cup Winners' Cup?

9. Which player won a Cup Winners' Cup medal in 1970, when he came on as substitute, and winners' medals in the European Cup in 1979 and 1980?

10. Who was the eighteen-year-old who headed an eighty-seventh-minute goal in Turin, to ensure victory over Juventus and a place for Arsenal in the 1980 final, for which he, however, was not selected?

74 The FA Cup – Players

1. Which player, in 1987, appeared in his fifth FA Cup Final in sixteen years?

2. Who is the only player to have appeared in five FA Cup Finals at Wembley, all for the same club?

3. Who has played in an FA Cup Final at Wembley in three different decades?

4. Johnny Giles played in four FA Cup Finals for Leeds United between 1965 and 1973, but for which club was he playing when he first appeared in the final?

5. Who played in three FA Cup Finals in the 1950s, each time with a different club?

6. Who was the first player after the Second World War to play against a club in the FA Cup Final one year and then play for them in the following year's final?

7. Who is the only player to have gained an FA Cup winner's medal both before and after the Second World War?

8. Who gained FA Cup losers' medals both before and after the Second World War, with Preston North End in 1937 and with Liverpool in 1950?

9. Who was the only Tottenham player to gain FA Cup winners' medals in 1961, 1962 and 1967?

10. Who gained FA Cup losers' medals with Sheffield United in 1936 and with Huddersfield Town in 1938?

75 Leading Football League Goalscorers in One Season

1. Who scored fifty-two goals for Peterborough in Division IV in 1960/61, the club's first season in the Football League?

2. Which player was the leading goalscorer in Division III in 1982/83 and in Division I in 1984/85?

3. Who was the eighteen-year-old who scored twenty-eight goals in Division II in 1979/80?

4. Which two Blackpool players led the Division II goalscorers in the consecutive seasons 1976/77 and 1977/78?

5. Which club provided the leading goalscorer in Division I in the consecutive seasons 1953/54 and 1954/55 and also in 1969/70 and 1970/71?

6. Who scored forty-six goals for Sheffield Wednesday in Division II in 1951/52, later returning to manage the club?

7. Which current international is the only player to have been leading goalscorer in Division I in two consecutive seasons, whilst playing for two different clubs?

8. Who was the leading goalscorer in Division II in 1960/61 and then in Division I in 1961/62?

9. Who is the only player to have scored more than forty Division I goals in a post-war season?

10. Who was the thirty-six-year-old who scored thirty-three First Division goals for Arsenal in 1947/48?

76 England Players with One Cap

1. Who scored for England on his début in January 1986, in a 4–0 victory over Egypt in Cairo, but has not since been selected for his country?

2. Which Aston Villa forward won his only England cap as a late second-half substitute against Wales at Wembley in May 1975, having just enough time to set up an equalizing goal?

3. Which current First Division manager made his only appearance for England in a European Nations Cup match against Malta in February 1971?

4. Which recently deposed manager became the first new cap selected by Sir Alf Ramsey after the 1966 World Cup success, making his only appearance against Spain at Wembley in May 1967, when he was twenty years old?

5. Which recent First Division manager won his only cap as England's centre-half against Northern Ireland at Wembley in November 1959?

6. Who was the Tottenham Hotspur winger who had the misfortune to make his England début in the 6–3 drubbing by Hungary at Wembley in November 1953, and was never selected again?

7. Which goalkeeper won his only cap as a substitute for Peter Shilton, against Australia in Melbourne in June 1983?

8. Which Brighton and Hove Albion forward made his only international appearance as a substitute against Australia, in Sydney in May 1980?

9. In the game mentioned in question 8, which Arsenal forward made his début and was replaced by the Brighton player – probably the only instance of one débutant being substituted for another and neither being capped again?

10. Which Luton Town forward was replaced by Tony Woodcock when making his international début in the 2–0 defeat by France in Paris in February 1984, and has never been selected for England again?

77 Scottish Football

1. Which club suffered its first defeat in twenty-seven league games in the last match of the 1985/86 season, and was pipped on goal difference for the Premier Division championship by a Celtic team which won its final game 5–0?

2. Which club finished the 1985/86 Premier Division season with just thirty-five points from thirty-six matches, its lowest total since 1951?

3. Who, in November 1984, scored a hat-trick for Celtic in their 7–1 win over St Mirren, his former club, so becoming the first player to score 100 goals in the Scottish Premier Division?

4. Who was the seventeen-year-old captain of Falkirk, who was transferred to Coventry City in March 1978?

5. Which thirty-three-year-old made his début for Scotland's under-21 side against East Germany in 1982/83?

6. Which club holds the record for most league goals in a season in Scotland, 142 in thirty-four matches, when it won the Second Division championship in 1937/38?

7. Which Partick Thistle forward won a Scottish League Cup winner's medal in a shock 4–1 victory over Celtic in October 1971, and a Football League Division II championship medal the following May, when he had been transferred to Norwich City?

8. Which Dundee United defender was the only player from a Scottish club to appear in the home international match against England at Wembley in May 1979?

9. Which club won the Scottish Division I championship in 1985/86, gaining promotion to the Premier Division for the first time?

10. Who scored 397 league goals for Celtic between 1922 and 1938, a record that is unlikely ever to be surpassed?

1. Which Fourth Division outfit proved themselves good treble-chance bankers when they drew their first six away matches in 1986/87, ending with thirteen draws from twenty-three away games, to add to eleven away draws in the previous season?

2. In November 1986, which twenty-five-year-old full-back achieved the unenviable distinction of being sent off for the tenth time in his career?

3. Which World Cup striker won the Golden Ball Award as European Footballer of the Year in 1986, the first player of his nationality to win the award for eleven years?

4. Who scored four penalties in four days against Coventry City in November 1986 – a hat-trick in a Littlewoods Cup fourth-round replay and then one in a Division I match?

5. Which team won the World Club Championship in December 1986, gaining a 1–0 victory over Steaua Bucharest, the European Cup holders?

6. Who captained England for the first time in November 1986, in a 2–0 victory in a European Championship qualifying game against Yugoslavia at Wembley?

7. Who were the two brothers, sons of a footballing father, who were both sent off in April 1986, when playing for Colchester United against Crewe Alexandra in a Division IV match?

8. Who, in March 1986, scored the goal that gave England victory over the USSR in Tbilisi, so ending a run of eighteen home games without defeat for the Soviets?

9. Who was the Liverpool-born player selected by the new Eire manager, Jack Charlton, to play against Wales in March 1986, after it had been confirmed that his great-grandmother was Irish?

10. Which player, having been forced into early retirement when he was at Everton, was registered to play for Manchester United in February 1986, but only on repayment of £58,000 insurance compensation?

79 *Football League – Multi-club Players*

1. Which current player, now with his fifth club, made more than one hundred appearances for each of his first four clubs, and also played international football whilst with all four?

2. Which player, in the 1979/80 season, achieved the unusual distinction of being leading goalscorer for two different clubs, with seventeen goals in twenty-four appearances for Portsmouth between August 1979 and February 1980, and then ten in sixteen games for Aldershot?

3. Which player played in all four divisions of the Football League within a twelve-month period in 1957/58, with Everton, Liverpool, Crewe Alexandra and Bury?

4. Who, in a career with Cardiff City, Derby County and Shrewsbury Town, achieved the feat of playing on all ninety-two Football League grounds, when he appeared at Port Vale in 1976?

5. Who played, and scored, for Colchester United, Birmingham City, Wrexham, Plymouth Argyle and Millwall in the same season, 1982/83?

6. Who topped the Second Division goalscoring chart for Grimsby Town in 1949/50 and for Blackburn Rovers in 1954/55, having spent periods in between with Coventry City and Birmingham City?

7. Who scored League hat-tricks for Luton Town in Division IV in 1965/66, for Middlesbrough in Division III in 1966/67 and Division II in 1967/68, and for Coventry City in Division I in 1969/70?

8. Who had scored for nine different clubs when he ended his Football League career at Rochdale in 1980?

9. Who scored a hat-trick for Blackburn Rovers against Everton at Goodison Park in November 1963, and later in the season, on the same ground, scored a hat-trick for Everton against Nottingham Forest?

10. Who was leading goalscorer in Division II in 1946/47 as a Newcastle United player, leading scorer again in 1948/49 with Southampton, and leading goalscorer in Division I in 1952/53 with Preston North End?

80 *Transfer Trail*

1. Which forward was transferred from Chelsea to Brighton and Hove Albion for £195,000 in November 1977, and scored sixteen goals in a two-year spell with the club before moving on to Fulham for £150,000, both transfer deals being records for the Sussex club?

2. When Leighton James joined Queen's Park Rangers from Derby County in October 1977, which international midfield player went the other way in a straight swap?

3. Which player did Coventry City sign from Bristol City for £325,000 in July 1979, selling him to the North American League side, Portland Timbers, for £365,000 only seven months later?

4. Who was bought by Nottingham Forest for £450,000 in June 1979 and sold to Everton for £400,000, less than two months later?

5. Which British player appeared in the Belgian League for RFC Bruges between July 1976 and December 1977, signing for £135,000 and returning to the Football League with Leicester City for the equivalent of £250,000?

6. Which Scotland international, scorer of a Scottish FA Cup Final hat-trick, signed for Luton Town in June 1976 but played only seventeen games in the Football League before signing for Partick Thistle in April 1977?

7. Who set the precedent for the recent influx of non-Scottish born players to Glasgow Rangers, when he moved from Mansfield Town for £90,000 in May 1981?

8. Which highly rated current international midfield player was released by West Ham United on a free transfer, moving to London neighbours Fulham in July 1982?

9. Who began a fitful career in the Scottish League when he moved from Fulham to Hibernian in November 1979 for a fee of £50,000?

10. Which player signed for Liverpool two days after Ian Rush, at a transfer valuation of some £30,000 higher than the former Chester striker, but was to play in only fourteen first-team games for the Merseysiders (without scoring a goal), before being transferred to Luton Town in April 1982 for £100,000?

81 *The Inter-Cities Fairs Cup/European Fairs Cup/UEFA Cup – Mixed Bag*

1. Which British player scored fourteen goals in one UEFA Cup tournament?

2. Which British club won the last European Fairs Cup in 1970/71, beating Juventus in the final on the 'away goals' rule?

3. Which club beat Leeds United 2–1 in September 1971 to take permanent possession of the European Fairs Cup?

4. Which British club remained undefeated in the UEFA Cup in 1972/73, but lost out to Liverpool in the semi-final on the 'away goals' rule?

5. Which club ended six years of domination by English teams by beating Tottenham Hotspur in the 1974 UEFA Cup Final?

6. Which club, when retaining the Inter-Cities Fairs Cup in 1962/63, defeated Celtic, Dunfermline Athletic and Hibernian in the first three rounds?

7. Who scored a total of four goals for Liverpool in the UEFA Cup Finals of 1973 and 1976?

8. Which club was beaten 3–2 on aggregate by Tottenham Hotspur in the 1971/72 UEFA Cup Final, the only European club final to have involved two Football League teams?

9. What was the name of the composite side that met Barcelona in the inaugural Inter-Cities Fairs Cup Final in 1958?

10. Which British club suffered its worst defeat in a European club match when it lost 4–0 to Lierse SK in Belgium, in the first round of the 1971/72 UEFA Cup?

82 World Cup—Mixed Bag

1. Who were the brothers who won World Cup winner's medals in 1966?

2. Who were the brothers who played for West Germany in the 1982 World Cup Final?

3. Who were the identical twins who played for Holland in the 1978 World Cup Final?

4. Which country was the first to be eliminated from a World Cup tournament without losing a match?

5. Which was the only country to avoid defeat in the 1978 World Cup tournament?

6. Who made his 100th international appearance in his country's opening game of the 1982 World Cup tournament, against Poland?

7. Who ended the 1982 competition with 103 international appearances, including twenty in three World Cup tournaments, during which he scored ten goals?

8. Which country provided the World Cup shock of 1966 by beating Italy 1–0 at Ayresome Park, Middlesbrough, and qualifying for the quarter-finals?

9. Which country, in 1982, in its first appearance in a World Cup tournament, was narrowly eliminated after the group matches, despite being undefeated and holding Italy, the eventual winners, to a 1–1 draw?

10. Which African country, on its first appearance in a World Cup tournament in 1978, beat Mexico 3–1 in its opening match, and in the final group game held West Germany, the holders, to a goalless draw?

83 *Scots Managers in England*

1. Which Manchester City wing-half made one international appearance for Scotland in 1934, and in 1946 began an association with one of England's most illustrious clubs, as manager and latterly as director, which has lasted for more than forty years?

2. Who was the Scottish wing-half who won five caps whilst playing for Preston North End before his name became inextricably linked with Liverpool FC?

3. Who was the Scottish wing-half who won twenty-five caps whilst playing for Preston North End and Arsenal, and subsequently managed at least seven different English League clubs, including the Manchester United team which won the 1977 FA Cup Final?

4. Who is the current manager of Leeds United, who played 586 League matches for the club between 1959 and 1976, and won fifty-four caps for Scotland?

5. Who is the current manager of Arsenal, who played 227 League games for the club, scoring sixty goals, between 1966 and 1972 and also made twelve appearances for Scotland?

6. Who was the 'craggy' Glaswegian who retired from a second term as manager of Notts County at the end of the 1986/87 season, having reached pensionable age earlier in the year?

7. Which Scot, a great wing-half with Tottenham Hotspur in the 1960s, succeeded Brian Clough as manager of Derby County, and led the club to the League championship in 1974/75?

8. Which Scottish winger gained fourteen caps between 1933 and 1938 while a player with Derby County, and won an FA Cup winner's medal with them in 1946 at the age of thirty-six, before turning to management and leading Blackburn Rovers to an FA Cup Final?

9. Which Dunfermline-born former Football League player was Third Division Manager of the Year in 1980/81, when he led Rotherham United to the divisional title, and Fourth Division Manager of the Year in 1981/82, when he did the same with Sheffield United?

10. Which Football League club did the former Liverpool and Scotland forward, Ian St John, once manage?

84 *The European Championships*

1. Which country, between 1960 and 1972, played in three of the first four European Championship Finals, and on the other occasion reached the semi-final?

2. Who was the secretary of the French Football Federation who gave his name to the European Championship trophy?

3. Which country won the 1964 European Nations Cup in front of 120,000 spectators?

4. Which of the UK nations did not take part in the qualifying matches for the European Championship before the 1968 tournament?

5. In which staging of the European Championships did the home international championship results over two seasons determine the United Kingdom's representative in the quarter-finals?

6. Which country won a European Championship Final after a replay?

7. Which country beat England 3–1 at Wembley in a quarter-final leg of the 1972 European Championships?

8. Who was the blond West German who was outstanding in midfield in the 1972 European Championships?

9. Which was the only UK nation to qualify for the 1976 European Championships, losing 3–1 on aggregate to Yugoslavia in the quarter-finals?

10. Which country failed to reach the final of the 1980 European Championships, despite not conceding a goal in its three group matches?

85 *Mixed Bag*

1. Which Third Division club fielded the same eleven players for their first twenty-eight League games in 1977/78, before John James replaced the injured Bobby Tynan for the 2–1 home victory over Hereford United which put them at the top of the table?

2. Between 1971 and 1977, who made 350 successive first-team appearances as Wrexham's goalkeeper before being transferred to local rivals Chester?

3. Who was the eighteen-year-old replacement for the in-eligible Peter Shilton who kept goal for Nottingham Forest in the 1978 League Cup Final, the first player ever to appear in a final at Wembley before making his League début?

4. Who was booked for the first time in 849 first-team games for his one and only club in the course of the 1978 Football League Cup Final replay at Old Trafford?

5. Who was the only player to represent Wimbledon in their début season in the First Division in 1986/87, who had also been with the club in 1977/78, their début season in the Football League?

6. Who played his 200th League game in April 1978 at the age of twenty-one years and three weeks – the youngest player ever to achieve this feat?

7. Who is the former Leicester City and Southampton centre-half who has more recently enjoyed comparative success as coach to the Iceland national team?

8. Which former Portsmouth defender resigned as the manager of Eire in October 1985, following a 2–0 defeat in Moscow?

9. Who was carried off with a broken shin-bone in an FA Cup semi-final in April 1986, so ending his hopes of making the England squad for that year's World Cup?

10. Who resigned as manager of Fourth Division Southend United in April 1986, after less than two years in the job?

86 *The FA Cup – Goalscorers*

1. Who scored the only goal of an FA Cup Final in the 1970s and almost immediately had to be substituted, reputedly because of emotional exhaustion?

2. Who was the twenty-one-year-old, signed earlier in the season from Fourth Division Rochdale, who scored both West Ham United's goals in the 1975 FA Cup Final?

3. Who was the only player to score in two different FA Cup Finals in the 1970s?

4. Which player in 1983 became the first captain to score in an FA Cup Final since Tottenham Hotspur's Danny Blanchflower, twenty-one years previously?

5. Who scored for Manchester City in successive FA Cup Finals in 1955 and 1956?

6. Which famous footballing personality scored two goals for Leicester City in their 3–1 semi-final victory over Portsmouth in 1949, but spent Cup Final day in hospital after a haemorrhage?

7. Which two players opposed each other in an FA Cup Final in the 1950s, but subsequently played on the same side in a final in the 1960s?

8. Who set an individual record for an FA Cup tie, with nine goals against Margate in a first-round match in 1971/72?

9. Who, playing for Birmingham City in 1956, was the last Welshman before Ian Rush in 1986 to score a goal in an FA Cup Final?

10. Who was the first player to score in two post-war FA Cup Finals?

87 Football League Players

1. Who won a Second Division championship medal with Newcastle United in 1964/65 and a First Division championship medal with Nottingham Forest in 1977/78?

2. Who scored 159 League goals for Middlesbrough in 415 matches, and was leading goalscorer in Division II for three seasons out of four between 1967/68 and 1970/71?

3. Which much-travelled forward scored exactly half of Third Division Plymouth Argyle's sixty-two League goals in 1984/85?

4. Who scored the only goal in the 1971 Charity Shield as a teenage full-back with Leicester City, but did not score in the Football League until March 1985, when he converted a penalty for Mansfield Town against Hereford United?

5. Who was the part-time professional with Rotherham United and later Nottingham Forest who became the first post-war footballer to score more than 200 League goals?

6. Who scored a total of fourteen goals for Hull City in nine consecutive Fourth Division matches, during a five-week period in the season 1981/82?

7. Which English international made more than 300 League appearances for two different clubs, in a playing career which began in 1958 and ended in 1975?

8. Who became the first substitute to score a hat-trick in a Football League match, netting three times for Birmingham City against Huddersfield Town in Division II in September 1968, having come on in the second half?

9. Who survived the Munich air crash and went on to make 567 League appearances for Manchester United?

10. Who scored two goals for each side in the First Division match between Aston Villa and Leicester City in March 1976?

88 Wales and Northern Ireland in the Final Stages of the World Cup

1. Who scored for Northern Ireland direct from a free kick, after only five minutes of their opening game with Algeria in the 1986 World Cup tournament?

2. Which Northern Ireland footballer gained the press accolade of 'outstanding British player' in the 1982 tournament?

3. Which Northern Ireland player was sent off in the 1982 World Cup match against the host nation, Spain?

4. Who scored five of Northern Ireland's six goals in the 1958 World Cup tournament?

5. Which country was twice beaten by Northern Ireland in the 1958 tournament?

6. Who was the inspiring captain of Northern Ireland in 1958?

7. Who were the two brothers who played for Wales in the 1958 World Cup tournament?

8. Which country did Wales beat in a play-off to qualify for the 1958 quarter-finals, having drawn with the same country in their opening match of the tournament?

9. Who scored twice for Wales in the 1958 tournament, so becoming the only Welshman to score more than one goal in the final stages of a World Cup competition?

10. Who was the Welsh goalkeeper who conceded only four goals in five matches during the 1958 tournament?

89 The European Cup – Clubs

1. Which club avenged the previous year's semi-final defeat by beating the holders, Steaua Bucharest, in the second round of the 1986/87 competition?

2. Which club, with a 2–1 victory over Bayern Munich in Vienna, were the surprise winners of the 1986/87 final?

3. Which Scottish club, competing in the European Cup for the first time in 1984, beat both Standard Liège and Rapid Vienna before losing 3–2 on aggregate to AS Roma in the semi-final?

4. Who beat the holders, Aston Villa, by five goals to two on aggregate in the quarter-final of the 1982/83 competition?

5. Which club was undefeated in its first thirteen matches in the European Cup before, surprisingly, losing at home to Dynamo Berlin in the 1980 quarter-finals?

6. Which club beat Liverpool, both home and away, in the second round of the 1974 competition?

7. Which British club surprisingly lost to the Turkish side, Fenerbahce, in the first round of the 1969 competition?

8. Which British club reached the semi-final in each of its first three appearances in the competition, and ended up as winners at the fourth attempt?

9. Which club set a record for the competition with an 18–0 aggregate win over Stade Dudelange of Luxemburg in the preliminary round of the 1966 European Cup?

10. Which British club won its first European Cup tie by an aggregate of 14–1?

90 *Internationals – Mixed Bag*

1. Who, in September 1946, played for Northern Ireland against England in Belfast, and, just two days later, for Eire against England in Dublin?

2. Which brothers, between 1946 and 1948, both played soccer and rugby for Ireland?

3. Who made his League début for Manchester City in 1975 as a seventeen-year-old, and between 1977 and 1983 played a record twenty-two games for the England under-21 team?

4. Who is the only player to have represented England at every level from schoolboy to full international, including amateur internationals?

5. Which club provided both centre-halves for the England–Wales match at Roker Park, Sunderland, in November 1950, each making their international débuts for their respective countries.

6. Which goalkeeper, in April 1959, became the first player from a Fourth Division club to play in an international match, when he made his solitary appearance for Wales against Northern Ireland?

7. Who, in the game against Czechoslovakia at Wembley in November 1978, became the first black footballer to play for England?

8. Who, between 1952 and 1962, played for his country in a record thirty-three consecutive home international championship matches?

9. Who was the England reserve, later to play in twenty-five full internationals for England, who made his international début in 1943 for Wales, in the second-half of a wartime game at Wembley?

10. Who was the Middlesbrough full-back who captained England throughout his international career, the first thirteen matches after the Second World War?

91 *Long-serving Football League Players*

1. Which midfield player made his League début in 1967, as a seventeen-year-old with Hartlepool United, and played under the management of Brian Clough in all four Divisions of the League before joining Bolton Wanderers in 1982?

2. Which wing-half made 775 League appearances for Manchester City and Chester between 1959 and 1981, joining Port Vale as a non-contracted player in 1983, when he was forty?

3. For which Third Division club did Ray Clemence play forty-eight League games before his transfer to Liverpool in 1967?

4. Which England forward began his League career with Huddersfield Town in 1966 and scored his 200th League goal almost twenty years later, when playing for Tranmere Rovers?

5. Who was the popular defender who made his League début with Leyton Orient in 1964, and was still registered as a player in the early 1980s, when he was manager of AFC Bournemouth?

6. For which First Division club did John Atyeo make two League appearances – as an amateur – before being transferred to Bristol City in 1951?

7. With which club did Billy Bonds begin his League career, before commencing his twenty years on the playing staff at West Ham United?

8. Between 1968 and 1980, who made more than 100 League appearances respectively for York City, Bournemouth, Norwich City and Southampton?

9. Which Yorkshire-born centre-forward began his League career with Halifax Town in 1959, finishing it in 1974 at Chesterfield, his ninth different League club?

10. Which Newcastle-born midfield player made more than 200 League appearances for both Swindon Town and Burnley, before ending his playing career with Blackpool in 1982, at thirty-eight years of age?

92 Record Transfers

1. Who signed for Tottenham Hotspur in May 1980 for £800,000, a record not only for the club, but also for any player leaving the Scottish league?

2. Who was transferred from Bolton Wanderers to Newcastle United for £85,000 in October 1966, a record for the Lancashire club which was to stand for more than thirteen years until November 1979, when Frank Worthington was sold to Birmingham City?

3. Which player, signed by Newcastle United for a record £225,000 in August 1978 and sold for £500,000, also a record, in May 1980, won a League championship medal both with the club he came from and with the one he moved to?

4. Ipswich Town's successive record signings in September 1971, October 1976 and January 1980 were all from clubs outside the First Division – which were the players who came respectively from Blackburn Rovers for £70,000, Plymouth Argyle for £240,000 and Millwall for £250,000?

5. Who was bought by Leeds United from Blackburn Rovers in March 1979 for £357,000 – not only their own record buy, but also a record for any British full-back?

6. Who became Britain's second most expensive footballer, after Trevor Francis, when he signed for Manchester City in June 1979 at a fee of £765,000?

7. Which player did Chelsea sign from a Scottish club in July 1974, the fee of £225,000 remaining a club record until April 1986, when they returned to Scotland for the purchase of Gordon Durie from Hibernian for £381,500?

8. Sunderland broke their transfer record three times in consecutive months at the end of 1979, successively signing which players from Hull City, Middlesbrough and San Lorenzo for £200,000, £300,000 and £320,000 respectively?

9. Which future Scottish international became Aston Villa's first £100,000 player in July 1969, being subsequently sold to Derby County in February 1974 for double the price?

10. Which player surpassed the West Ham United record sale figure, set by Martin Peters in March 1970, when he moved to Birmingham City for £225,000 in June 1979?

93 England Players

1. When twenty-year-old Bobby Charlton made the first of his 106 appearances for England in April 1958, which twenty-eight-year-old Fulham full-back won the first of three consecutive caps, as a replacement for the Munich disaster victim, Roger Byrne?

2. Which two players linked with Billy Wright to form a Wolverhampton Wanderers half-back line for England's three group matches in the 1958 World Cup?

3. Which twenty-five-year-old amateur international was transferred from Bishop Auckland to Manchester United in November 1958 and, within a year, scored against Italy on the first of his three appearances for England as a professional?

4. Who scored sixteen goals for England in nineteen matches before losing his life in the Munich plane crash?

5. Who was Brian Clough's Middlesbrough team-mate, who joined him as a débutant in England's forward line for the drawn game with Wales in 1959?

6. Who won five caps for England in 1959/60 whilst playing for Hibernian, adding three more in 1965/66 after he had moved south to Arsenal?

7. Which Nottingham Forest centre-forward, on his début, scored both of England's goals against Wales at Wembley in November 1964, but was permanently discarded after the following match, against the Netherlands in Amsterdam?

8. Which player began his twenty-eight-cap, nine-year international career in December 1965 as a substitute – the first England player to win his first cap as a replacement?

9. Which two players on their international débuts joined Emlyn Hughes to form an all-Liverpool half-back line for England against Wales, at Wembley in May 1971.

10. Who were England's two new full-backs in the 1–1 draw with Yugoslavia in October 1972, one who ended his international career ten years later with forty-two caps, the other who made just one more appearance, almost eight years later, against Australia in Sydney in June 1980?

94 World Cup—Mixed Bag

1. Who played for Spain in the 1962 World Cup after playing for Hungary in the 1954 tournament?

2. Who was the nineteen-year-old who scored two goals for Brazil in the 1958 World Cup, before being replaced by Pele, and then went on to play for Italy in the 1962 tournament?

3. Who is the only player to have represented two different countries in a World Cup Final – representing Argentina in 1930 and Italy in 1934?

4. Which country, with a 3–2 victory in 1950, was the first to beat Italy in a World Cup tournament?

5. Which country, in 1954, became the first to beat Uruguay in a World Cup tournament?

6. In which newly built stadium was a World Cup Final played before nearly 200,000 spectators?

7. Which football administrator had his name engraved on the first World Cup trophy, which was won outright by Brazil in 1970?

8. Who was the Newcastle United player who led the Chilean attack against England in the 1950 World Cup tournament?

9. Who was sent on as a substitute for Poland after eighty-three minutes of their second-round match against Brazil in the 1986 tournament, so equalling Uwe Seeler's record of twenty-one appearances in the final stages of the competition?

10. Who, at seventeen years and one month, was the youngest footballer to play in a World Cup tournament?

95 Football League—Mixed Bag

1. Which current First Division club has played in all six divisions of the Football League – the four divisions as currently constituted, and, in addition, Third Division South and North?

2. Who was the first player to win separate League championships with the same club as a player and as a manager?

3. Which current First Division side had both its record League win and its record League defeat against Loughborough Town; winning 12–0 in Division II in March 1900, and losing 8–0, also in Division II, in December 1896?

4. Who, in October 1936, celebrated his seventeenth birthday with a hat-trick for Burnley against Tottenham Hotspur, on his League début?

5. Which club won the Division II championship by a record fifteen points in 1973/74?

6. Which club finished in the bottom two in the Fourth Division for five seasons in succession from 1960 to 1964, applying for re-election each time?

7. Who set a record by scoring every one of his 357 Football League goals in the First Division?

8. Whose 379 League goals, scored between 1923 and 1939, included thirty-seven hat-tricks?

9. Which future international scored for Brighton and Hove Albion in March 1976, in the first minute of his first Football League match?

10. Who was the future England cap who became player-manager of Carlisle United in 1946, at twenty-three years of age, and three years later transferred himself to Sunderland for £18,000?

96 *International Players Worldwide*

1. Who was still captain and centre-back of the Danish national football team in 1988, at thirty-eight years of age?

2. Who was the Swedish defender officially recognized as the world's most capped player, with 115 international appearances, until his record was overtaken by Pat Jennings in 1986?

3. Who is the flying Soviet winger, a former European Footballer of the Year, who in 1986 became the first USSR player to make 100 international appearances?

4. Who was the Anderlecht midfield star of the late 1960s and early 1970s who set a record of eighty-one international appearances for Belgium?

5. Who was the famous 'strolling' Austrian centre-back of the 1950s, who won sixty-two caps?

6. Who was the giant Czechoslovakian centre-back who played a prominent role in his country's success at the 1976 European Championships, scoring at both ends in the 3–1 semi-final victory over Holland?

7. Which Borussia Moenchengladbach full-back played ninety-six times for West Germany, but found Liverpool's Kevin Keegan more than a handful in the 1977 European Cup Final?

8. Who was the Brazilian forward of the 1970s, he of the deadly left foot, who played 108 times for his country?

9. Who was the Peruvian sweeper who, according to unconfirmed sources, played in 127 international matches during the 1960s and 1970s?

10. Who was the tall, commanding left full-back who captained both Inter Milan, to European Cup success, and Italy, to the 1970 World Cup Final, in the course of a career in which he was capped ninety-seven times?

97 European Competitions – Mixed Bag

1. Which Liverpool player scored his first hat-trick for the club in the 6–0 European Super Cup victory over SV Hamburg in 1977?

2. Which British player is the only one to have scored in both a European Fairs Cup and a UEFA Cup Final?

3. Which British player has been the competition's leading scorer in both the Inter-Cities Fairs Cup and the European Cup?

4. Which is the only club to have won the European Cup, the Cup Winners' Cup and the UEFA Cup?

5. Which is the only club to have won the UEFA Cup and the European Cup in successive seasons?

6. Which club won the first two annual European Super Cup matches, involving the winners of the European Cup and Cup Winners' Cup?

7. Which was the first British club to reach the final of all three European cup competitions?

8. Who are the only two players to have appeared for Liverpool in the final of all three European cup competitions?

9. Which country has been the most successful in the three European competitions, providing a total of twenty-two trophy winners?

10. Which is the only Scottish club to have won the European Super Cup?

98 *World Cup Referees and Linesmen*

1. Who was the Brazilian who refereed the 1986 final between Argentina and West Germany?

2. Who was the English referee who awarded a penalty to both sides in the 1974 final?

3. Which British referee disallowed a goal for Brazil, direct from a corner, in a 1978 World Cup match with Sweden, because he had blown for full-time before the ball entered the net?

4. Who was the Swiss referee who credited England with a goal in the 1966 final after Geoff Hurst's famous extra-time shot had come down off the underside of the crossbar?

5. Who was the West German referee who sent off Antonio Rattin, Argentina's captain, in the quarter-final match with England in the 1966 tournament?

6. Which English referee sent off two Uruguayans in the 1966 quarter-final match with West Germany at Hillsborough?

7. Who was the English referee in charge of the appalling match between Chile and Italy in the 1962 tournament, which became infamous as 'the Battle of Santiago'?

8. Who was the Welsh linesman who raised his flag for offside as Ferenc Puskas put the ball in the net for what would have been an equalizing goal for Hungary, in the dying minutes of the 1954 final?

9. Which English referee, in the 1954 World Cup, sent off three players and awarded two penalties in the 'Battle of Berne' between Brazil and Hungary?

10. Who was the Belgian referee who had charge of the first World Cup Final, between Uruguay and Argentina, on 30 July 1930?

99 FA Cup—Mixed Bag

1. Where was the FA Cup Final played immediately before Wembley was first used in 1923?

2. Who captained the Arsenal team that won the Cup in 1950 and managed Manchester City when they lifted the trophy in 1969?

3. Who captained Aston Villa, the 1920 winners, and subsequently managed Sheffield Wednesday, 4–2 winners over West Bromwich Albion in the 1935 final, and Nottingham Forest, 2–1 winners over Luton Town in 1959?

4. Who played for Blackpool as an amateur in the 1951 final and, later in his career, as a professional, captained another club to victory in the competition?

5. Which team, in 1954–55, beat Bury in a third-round tie which lasted nine hours and twenty-two minutes, spread over five games, all played on different grounds?

6. Which famous Football League side failed to win any of its sixteen FA Cup matches, including replays, between 1952 and 1963?

7. Who won an FA Cup winner's medal with Newcastle United in 1924, at forty-one years of age?

8. Who was sent off in two FA Cup ties in 1980 whilst playing for Everton, having twelve years previously been sent off in the competition as a Manchester United player?

9. Which is the only Football League club to have been drawn to play FA Cup matches against clubs from all four home countries?

10. Which club has achieved the unprecedented feat of reaching successive FA Cup Finals without being drawn at home, for any round, in either year?

100 *Football League Clubs*

1. Which club has never won the Football League championship, but was leading the First Division in September 1939 when League football was suspended at the outbreak of the Second World War, with a maximum six points from three matches?

2. Which club became the first to be relegated in each of three successive Football League seasons, when dropping from Division I to Division IV between 1979/80 and 1981/82?

3. Which club defeated the League champions, Everton, on the opening day of the 1985/86 season, their first Divison I victory on the first day of the season since 1959/60, when Everton again had been the victims?

4. Which Fourth Division club acquired Neville Southall on loan from Everton for nine League games at the end of the 1982/83 season, and went on to gain promotion?

5. Which club finished bottom of Division I in 1983/84, bottom of Division II in 1984/85, and ended the season 1985/86 above Swansea City at the bottom of Division III on goal difference only?

6. Which club finished bottom of Division I and II in the successive seasons 1967/68 and 1968/69?

7. Which club joined the Football League in 1923/24 in the Third Division South, and was in the Third Division for a record forty-seven consecutive years before being relegated at the end of the 1969/70 season, winning promotion the following season?

8. Which is the only club to have scored exactly eleven goals in a post-war Football League fixture, beating Southport 11–0 in Division IV on Boxing Day 1962?

9. Which club achieved its biggest ever League win with an 8–1 victory over Gateshead in Division IV in September 1958, but finished the season in twenty-second place and had to apply for re-election?

10. Which club finished in the first three in Division I in eight seasons out of nine between 1952/53 and 1960/61?

101 *1988—International Matches*

1. Who made his only England appearance to date in February, as a sixty-seventh-minute substitute in the goalless draw with Israel in Tel Aviv?

2. Who scored for both sides in the 2–2 friendly between England and Holland at Wembley in March 1988?

3. Which country contested the 1988 Rous Cup competition with England and Scotland?

4. Who was the only uncapped player in England's European Championship squad?

5. Which country, with a weakened team because of injuries to key players, gained a surprise 1–0 victory over Italy, who were playing a final 'warm-up' game before the European Championships?

6. Who scored the only goal of the England vs Republic of Ireland European Championship match?

7. Who scored a hat-trick for Holland to effectively eliminate England from the 1988 European Championships, and finished as the competition's leading scorer, with five goals in all?

8. Who were England's two goal scorers in the European Championship finals?

9. Who ended the European Championships, and maybe his international career, with ninety-nine caps to his credit?

10. Who hit the post and had a penalty saved with successive touches of the ball in the second half of the 1988 European Championship final?

102 *1988—Cup Competitions*

1. Who scored the only goal of the English FA Cup final?

2. Which non-League club drew 1–1 with Second Division Middlesbrough in their third round FA Cup tie?

3. Which two clubs, having been drawn together for a record fifteenth time in the FA Cup, needed three replays to decide their third round tie?

4. Who scored the only goal of the fourth round FA Cup match between Coventry City and Watford, to put the holders out of the competition?

5. Which Third Division club, with a reputation for FA Cup giant-killing, produced a shock 2–1 victory over Tottenham Hotspur in a fourth round match?

6. Which club, subsequently relegated from the Premier Division, defeated Glasgow Rangers 2–0 in a Scottish FA Cup tie?

7. Which club, subsequently relegated to Division III, were the surprising 4–1 winners over Luton Town in the Simod Cup final?

8. Which player gained a winner's medal in the 1988 Simod Cup, to add to the one he won in the 1986 Full Members cup, when a Chelsea player?

9. Who missed a penalty in the Littlewoods Cup final, which would have given his team a 3–1 lead?

10. Who was the Dutch player who, ironically, scored the goal that beat holders Ajax, Amsterdam, in the European Cup Winners Cup final, ensuring victory for Belgian club, Mechelen?

103 *1988—Mixed Bag*

1. Which English player made his début for Glasgow Rangers on 2nd January, in the traditional holiday fixture with Celtic, before a 60,800 Parkhead crowd?

2. Which leading European club dropped its first league point of the season in January, after seventeen successive wins?

3. Which former England International, forced into premature retirement through injury, announced a comeback with Johannesburg club Kaizer Chiefs?

4. Who became the subject of the first £1 million transfer deal between two Scottish clubs when he left St Mirren in February 1988?

5. Which former international played against Liverpool in the 1987/88 FA Cup final, having previously played against them in the final of another competition?

6. Who was fined and suspended for eight matches after being sent off for a record fifth time in one season?

7. Who became England's first Division II débutant since Alan Devonshire in 1980, making a favourable impression in the goal-less friendly against Hungry?

8. Who was Mike England's immediate successor as team manager of Wales, his temporary appointment lasting for just one match, a 2–1 home defeat at the hands of Yugoslavia?

9. Which two players successively broke the British transfer record for a goalkeeper, when moving in successive weeks for £750,000 and £850,000, respectively?

10. Which England International has returned to his former League club in a £250,000 transfer, after three years in Italy?

104 1988—Football League

1. Who scored the first League hat-trick of 1988 when Walsall beat Rotherham United 5–2 on 2nd January, was substituted during the second half, left the ground in a huff and, within weeks, had been transferred to Leicester City?

2. Who scored the only goal of the match, to end Liverpool's record-equalling unbeaten League run, in their thirtieth game of the season?

3. Who was the seventeen-year-old who scored a hat trick in Southampton's 4–2 win over Arsenal, his first full League appearance?

4. Which famous old club conceded 100 League goals in the 1987/88 season for the first time in its history?

5. Which club was relegated at the end of the 1987/88 season for the second year in succession?

6. Who, with 25 League goals, was the First Division's leading scorer during the 1987/88 season?

7. Who was the only player to score over thirty League goals in the 1987/88 season?

8. Which Fourth Division club missed the end-of-season promotion play-offs for the second year running, through losing its final League match to champions Wolverhampton Wanderers in 1988, and to relegation-threatened Burnley in 1987?

9. Who, at the end of the 1987/88 season, surpassed Terry Paine's record of 824 Football league appearances?

10. Which international player scored seven goals in the Barclay's League play-off matches at the end of the 1987/88 season?

ANSWERS

1 *The 1987/88 Season*

1. Andy Jones (Port Vale and Aldershot) 2. Nigel
Clough (Nottingham Forest) 3. Real Madrid 4. Atalanta
(of Bergamo) – who went on to reach the semi-final of the
competition.

5. Gary   Gillespie   (Liverpool)   6. Gary   Mackay
7. Yugoslavia   8. Aston Villa   9. Huddersfield Town
10. Ken Brown (Norwich City)

2 *Football League Clubs Nicknames*

1. Manchester United   2. West Bromwich Albion
3. Newcastle United and Notts County   4. (a) Brighton
and Hove Albion (b) Grimsby Town (c) Blackpool
5. (a)Norwich City (b) Sheffield Wednesday (c) Cardiff City
6. (a) Millwall (b) Hull City   7. Bolton Wanderers   8. (a)
Plymouth Argyle (b) Darlington   9. (a) Aston Villa (b) Port
Vale   10. (a) Brentford (b) Watford

3 *The 1986 Mexico World Cup Finals*

1. Pat Jennings (Northern Ireland)   2. Michel Platini
(France)   3. Gordon Strachan   4. Portugal   5. Ray
Wilkins   6. Poland   7. Peter Beardsley (against
Paraguay)   8. George Courtney   9. Igor Belanov
10. Emilio Butragueño

4 *Football League Division I – the 1980s*

1. Charlton Athletic   2. Wimbledon   3. Manchester
United   4. Coventry City   5. Stoke City   6. Norwich
City   7. Southampton   8. Watford   9. Manchester
United   10. Ipswich Town

5 *The European Cup – Goalscorers*

1. Richi Alonso   2. Peter Withe   3. Trevor Francis
4. Phil Neal (1977 against Borussia Moenchengladbach
and 1984 against AS Roma)   5. Alan Kennedy
6. Georg Schwarzenbeck   7. Johann Cruyff   8. Tommy
Gemmell (1967 against Inter Milan and 1970 against
Feyenoord)   9. Velibor Vasovic   10. Alfredo di Stefano

6 *The FA Cup – Non-league Giant-killers*
1. Caernarfon Town   2. Altrincham   3. Telford United
(1984 and 1985)   4. Burton Albion   5. Blyth Spartans
6. Harlow Town   7. Wimbledon   8. Worcester City
9. Yeovil Town   10. Hereford United

7 *Current Football League Managers*
1. Dave Bassett   2. Graham Carr   3. Brian Miller
4. Harry Redknapp   5. Lou Macari   6. Steve Coppell
7. Denis Smith   8. Howard Wilkinson   9. Chris Nicholl
10. Lennie Lawrence

8 *Football League Transfers*
1. Clive Allen   2. Bryan Robson (from West Bromwich to
Manchester United in October 1981)   3. Ian Wallace (from
Coventry)   4. Andy Gray (from Aston Villa to
Wolverhampton Wanderers)   5. David Mills (from
Middlesbrough to West Bromwich Albion)   6. Alan Ball
(Blackpool to Everton in 1966 and Everton to Arsenal in
1971)   7. Alan Clarke (Fulham to Leicester City for
£150,000 estimated in June 1968 and Leicester City to
Leeds United for £165,000 in July 1969)   8. Jimmy
Greaves (from A C Milan to Tottenham Hotspur)   9. Denis
Law (from Huddersfield Town to Manchester City)
10. Gerry Daly (from Manchester United to Derby County)

9 *Mixed Bag*
1. Wimbledon   2. John Mortimore   3. Leyton Orient
4. Maurice Johnston and Murdo McLeod   5. Mark Hateley
and Glenn Hoddle   6. David Williams   7. Tony Parks
8. Avi Cohen   9. Neil Webb (Nottingham Forest)   10.
Steve Perryman (Tottenham Hotspur)

10 *England in the Final Stages of the World Cup*
1. Bryan Robson   2. Viv Anderson   3. Mick Mills   4. Peter
Bonetti   5. Bobby Charlton   6. Allan Clarke   7. Eusebio
(from the penalty spot in the semi-final against Portugal)
8. Geoff Hurst   9. Uruguay   10. Jimmy Adamson

11 Goalscorers for England
1. Bobby Charlton   2. Gary Lineker   3. Steve Bloomer (Derby County)   4. Tommy Lawton   5. Wilf Mannion
6. Stan Mortensen   7. Jack Rowley   8. Jimmy Greaves
9. Dennis Wilshaw   10. Malcolm MacDonald

12 The Inter-cities Fairs Cup/The European Fairs Cup/The UEFA Cup – Clubs
1. Dundee United   2. Tottenham Hotspur (1984)   3. IFK Gothenburg   4. PSV Eindhoven   5. Bastia   6. Twente Enschede   7. Leeds United   8. Birmingham City
9. Dunfermline Athletic   10. Ferencvaros (Hungary)

13 Scottish Football
1. Heart of Midlothian   2. Clyde   3. Graeme Souness (Rangers)   4. Meadowbank Thistle   5. Dundee United
6. Alfie Conn   7. Bobby Lennox   8. John Greig
9. Kilmarnock   10. Motherwell

14 Football League – Leading Club Goalscorers
1. Craig Madden   2. Peter Lorimer   3. Mike Channon
4. Bobby Tambling   5. Kevin Hector (Derby County)
6. William 'Dixie' Dean   7. John Atyeo   8. Stuart Leary
9. Gordon Turner   10. George Camsell

15 Family Connections
1. Brian and Jimmy Greenhoff   2. Ian and Roger Morgan
3. Paul and Ron Futcher   4. Dave and John Hollins
5. George Eastham (Bolton Wanderers): one cap in 1935; George Eastham (Arsenal): nineteen caps 1963–66   6. Bill Dodgin (Snr) and Bill Dodgin (Jnr)   7. Bob Shankly – Dundee 1962; Bill Shankly – Liverpool 1964 and 1966 (and 1973)   8. Graham and Ray Wilkins (sons of George)
9. Tony Hateley (father of Mark)   10. Con and Mick Martin

16 Northern Ireland Internationals
1. Danny Blanchflower   2. Billy Bingham   3. Sammy McIlroy   4. Joe Bambrick   5. Peter Doherty   6. Jim Platt   7. Harry Gregg   8. Billy Hamilton   9. George Best   10. Terry Neill

17 World Cup—Mixed Bag
1. Dirk Nanninga (Holland)   2. Alessandro Altobelli
3. Zico   4. Robbie Rensenbrink (Holland)   5. Johan
Neeskens   6. Eusebio   7. Peter Shilton   8. Jan
Jongbloed   9. Gylmar (Brazil – 1958 and 1962)
10. Antonio Carbajal (Mexico)

18 The FA Cup – Clubs
1. Wimbledon   2. Arsenal (1978, 1979 and 1980)
3. Brighton and Hove Albion (1982/83)   4. Queen's Park
Rangers (1981/82)   5. Leicester City (1949, 1961, 1963
and 1969)   6. Manchester United (1947/48)   7. West
Ham United – being the Second Division club in 1923 and
1980, and playing Second Division opposition in 1964 and
1975   8. Bradford   9. Manchester City (1933 and
1934)   10. Tottenham Hotspur

19 Transfer Trail – England Internationals
1. Terry McDermott   2. Peter Taylor   3. Geoff Hurst
4. Peter Withe   5. Tony Morley   6. Chris Woods
7. Mike Pejic   8. Dave Thomas   9. Colin Viljoen
10. Stan Bowles

20 1987—Mixed Bag
1. Colin Addison, who became assistant manager to Ron
Atkinson at West Bromwich Albion   2. Chris Hemming
3. Paul Goddard   4. Gary Bailey (Manchester United)
5. Bob Latchford   6. Ian Wilson   7. Mansfield Town –
beating the holders, Bristol City, 5–4 on penalties after the
scores had finished at 1–1 after extra time   8. Liam
O'Brien   9. Hamilton Academicals   10. Chris Woods
(Glasgow Rangers)

21 The Football League Cup
1. Swindon Town   2. Leicester City   3. Derek Reeves
4. Gerry Hitchens   5. Rodney Marsh   6. Aston Villa and
Everton, in 1977   7. Alan Hardaker   8. Joe Mercer
9. George Eastham   10. Andy Gray

22 The European Cup Winners' Cup – Players

1. Andy Gray   2. John Hewitt   3. Brian Hall   4. Robbie Rensenbrink   5. Graham Rix   6. Peter Osgood   7. Carlos Reixach   8. Alan Sealey   9. Neil Young and Francis Lee (pen.)   10. Willie Johnston

23 Football League Clubs – Division II

1. Portsmouth   2. Oldham Athletic   3. Sunderland
4. Oxford United   5. Cambridge United   6. Birmingham City   7. West Ham United   8. Leicester City
9. Liverpool   10. Everton (1930/31 and 1931/32)

24 The European Championships

1. France   2. Michel Platini   3. Wales   4. Kevin Keegan   5. Horst Hrubesch   6. Wilfred Van Moer
7. Czechoslovakia   8. Gerd Müller (West Germany)
9. Albania   10. France

25 England Players

1. Trevor Smith (Birmingham City)   2. Brian Clough
3. Dave Watson (Sunderland, Manchester City, Werder Bremen, Southampton and Stoke City)   4. John Barnes
5. Phil Parkes   6. Paul Mariner   7. Jimmy Melia   8. Ian Callaghan   9. Stanley Matthews (September 1934–May 1957)   10. Tommy Lawton

26 Scotland in the Final Stages of the World Cup

1. David Speedie   2. Joe Jordan (1974, 1978 and 1982)
3. New Zealand   4. Holland, in 1978   5. Don Masson
6. Denis Law   7. Tommy Hutchison   8. Uruguay
9. Willie Ormond   10. Archie Gemmill

27 British Club Grounds

1. Exeter City (St James's Park)   2. Maine Road (Manchester City against Stoke City)   3. Aldershot and Chesterfield   4. Northampton Town and Swindon Town
5. Stirling Albion   6. Motherwell, Partick Thistle and Clyde   7. Goodison Park (Everton)   8. Hartlepool and Stoke   9. Cleethorpes   10. Queen's Park

28 Football League—Mixed Bag
1. Trevor Francis (for Birmingham City against Bolton Wanderers) 2. Neil Webb 3. Duncan Edwards 4. Neil McBain 5. Sir Stanley Matthews 6. Tony Coton
7. Paul Cooper 8. Cardiff City (Len Davies missed against Birmingham City in May 1924 and the Welsh club lost the title to Huddersfield Town on goal average) 9. Newport County 10. Len Shackleton

29 The FA Cup – Players
1. Brian Borrows 2. Kevin MacDonald 3. Wilf Rostron
4. Glenn Roeder 5. Mick Martin (West Bromwich Albion against Ipswich Town) 6. Roy Dwight (Elton John's cousin!) 7. Kevin Ratcliffe (Everton) 8. Martin Buchan
9. Roy Paul 10. Joe Smith

30 Mixed Bag
1. Joey Jones 2. Francis Lee (Manchester City) 3. Alun Evans 4. Scarborough and Wigan Athletic 5. Wigan Athletic 6. Gary Plumley 7. Dixie Dean 8. Aston Villa (Graham Turner and Billy McNeill) 9. Dave Bennett (for Manchester City in 1981) 10. Terry Butcher

31 Welsh Internationals
1. Andy Jones 2. Ian Edwards 3. John Toshack
4. Wyn Davies (Bolton Wanderers, Newcastle United, Manchester City, Manchester United and Blackpool)
5. Ivor Allchurch 6. Mel Charles 7. Trevor Ford
8. Des Palmer 9. Billy Meredith 10. Graham Moore

32 World Cup—Mixed Bag
1. Mexico 2. Brazil 3. Uruguay (1950) 4. Holland (1974) 5. West Germany (1954) 6. Bulgaria
7. England 8. Algeria 9. France 10. India

33 Football League Clubs – Mixed Bag
1. Tottenham Hotspur (the match was against the League champions, Everton, just five days before the F A Cup Final) 2. Port Vale 3. Peterborough United 4. Leeds United (Jeff Astle scored for West Bromwich Albion)
5. Manchester United 6. Southport 7. Thames
8. Ipswich Town 9. West Ham United 10. Birmingham City

34 The European Cup – Clubs
1. Barcelona 2. Aston Villa 3. Liverpool 4. Celtic (1967) 5. Jimmy Rimmer (substitute goalkeeper for Manchester United in 1968, and injured after eight minutes when playing for Aston Villa in 1982) 6. Barcelona
7. Benfica 8. Manchester United (1956/57)
9. Hibernian 10. Stade de Reims

35 Football League Transfers
1. Peter Beardsley (Newcastle United to Liverpool)
2. Brian McClair (Celtic to Manchester United) 3. Steve Daley (from Wolverhampton Wanderers to Manchester City for £1,437,500) 4. John Barton 5. Wilf Smith
6. Trevor Ford 7. Phil Parkes (from Queen's Park Rangers to West Ham for £565,000) 8. Bryn Jones 9. David Jack 10. Alf Common (in 1904, he had been the first player to be transferred for £500, joining Sunderland from Sheffield United)

36 England Caps
1. Billy Wright 2. Bob Crompton 3. Joe Mercer
4. Nobby Stiles (twenty-eight caps) 5. Raich Carter
6. Gerry Hitchens – against Switzerland in May 1962, when he was an Inter Milan player 7. Ronnie Clayton
8. Frank Swift 9. Emlyn Hughes 10. Neil Franklin

37 West Germany in the World Cup
1. Sepp Maier 2. Portugal 3. Karl-Heinz Rummenigge
4. Paul Breitner 5. Wolfgang Overath 6. Gerd Muller
7. Helmut Haller 8. Karl-Heinz Schnellinger 9. East Germany 10. Fritz and Otmar Walter

38 *Football League—Mixed Bag*
1. Jimmy Hill   2. Johnny Haynes (Fulham)   3. Gordon
Taylor   4. Terry Neill   5. Ron Atkinson   6. Alf Ramsey
7. Emlyn Hughes   8. Ron Harris (Chelsea)   9. Colin Bell
10. Len Shackleton

39 *The European Championships*
1. Denmark   2. Spain (against Malta)   3. Northern
Ireland   4. Spain   5. Allan Simonsen (Denmark)
6. Bernd Deitz   7. Klaus Allofs   8. England   9. 1976 (in
Yugoslavia)   10. 1968 (in Rome)

40 *Football League Goalscorers*
1. Trevor Senior   2. Gary Rowell   3. Bryan Robson
4. Tony Woodcock (Arsenal)   5. Jason Dozzell   6. Paul
Walsh   7. Jackie Balmer   8. Chris Lawler (Liverpool)
9. David Peach   10. Colin Clarke (Southampton)

41 *Football Awards*
1. Stanley Matthews   2. Clive Allen   3. Bert Trautmann
(1956)   4. Michel Platini   5. Denis Law (1964)
6. Kevin Keegan (1978 and 1979)   7. Thomas N'Komo
8. Ian Rush   9. Joe Harper (Aberdeen) and Francis Lee
(Manchester City)   10. Elias Figueroa

42 *Playing Days*
1. Mel Machin (Manchester City)   2. Graeme Souness
(Glasgow Rangers)   3. Colin Harvey (Everton)   4. George
Graham (Arsenal)   5. Bobby Gould (Wimbledon)   6. Terry
Yorath (Swansea City)   7. Howard Kendall (Athletico
Bilbao)   8. Joe Royle (Oldham Athletic)   9. John Duncan
(Ipswich Town)   10. Dave Mackay (Doncaster Rovers)

43 *Football League—Mixed Bag*
1. Ted Croker   2. Charlton Athletic   3. Gary Mills
4. Ray Wilkins   5. Tony Book   6. Dennis Mortimer, Des
Bremner and Gordon Cowans   7. Huddersfield Town
8. Portsmouth (1948/49 and 1949/50)   9. Hereford
United (1972/73)   10. Accrington

44 *The 1986 Mexico World Cup Finals*
1. John Barnes   2. Steve Nicol (Scotland)   3. France
4. Sammy McIlroy   5. Graeme Souness (Scotland)
6. Peter Shilton   7. Canada   8. Rudi Voller (West
Germany)   9. Jorge Burruchaga   10. Dr Carlos Bilardo

45 *The European Cup Winners' Cup – Clubs*
1. Wrexham   2. Ajax, Amsterdam   3. Everton   4. Rapid
Vienna   5. Linfield   6. Aberdeen   7. Glasgow Rangers
8. Slovan Bratislava   9. Tottenham Hotspur   10. A C
Fiorentina

46 *Mixed Bag*
1. Jimmy Melia   2. Andy King   3. Bournemouth
4. Stan Storton   5. Maurice Evans   6. Cambridge United
7. Brendon Batson   8. Bernard Joy (Corinthian Casuals)
9. Kevin Reeves   10. Malcolm Allison

47 *England Players*
1. Liverpool (Clemence, Neal, McDermott, Hughes, R.
Kennedy and Callaghan – plus Keegan, then with S V
Hamburg)   2. Arsenal (Bastin, Bowden, Copping, Drake,
Hapgood, Male and Moss)   3. Alan Mullery   4. Bill Perry
5. Colin Grainger   6. Jimmy Greaves   7. Mike O'Grady
8. Tommy Wright   9. Jeff Blockley   10. Tony Adams

48 *Football League—Mixed Bag*
1. Ken and Terry Hibbitt   2. Alec and David Herd
3. Arsenal   4. Everton   5. Denis Law   6. Jimmy Seed
7. Les Allen   8. Sunderland   9. Leeds United
10. Burnley

49 *World Cup Captains*
1. Bruce Rioch   2. Socrates   3. Martin O'Neill   4. Billy
Wright (1950, 1954 and 1958)   5. Dino Zoff (1982)
6. Kazimierz Deyna   7. Dave Bowen   8. Uwe Seeler
9. Giuseppe Meazza   10. Jose Nasazzi

50 *Scots in the Football League*
1. Charlie Aitken   2. Bobbie Collins (Leeds United)
3. Hughie Gallacher   4. Alex James   5. John Hewie
6. Willie Stevenson   7. Martin Buchan (Manchester United
1977, Aberdeen 1970)   8. Pat Crerand   9. Kenny Dalglish
(Liverpool and Celtic)   10. Frank McAvennie

51 *The FA Cup – Players*
1. Frank Stapleton (Arsenal in 1978, 1979 and 1980,
Manchester United in 1983 and 1985)   2. Paul Allen
(West Ham United)   3. Norman Whiteside (Manchester
United)   4. John Sissons   5. Howard Kendall   6. David
McCreery   7. Eddie Kelly   8. Dennis Clarke   9. Gary
Mabbutt   10. Bert Turner

52 *The European Cup – Mixed Bag*
1. Helmut Ducadam   2. Nigel Spink   3. Dynamo Kiev
4. Derry City   5. Leeds United (1969/70)   6. Francisco
Gento (Real Madrid 1956–66)   7. Raymond Kopa
8. Ferenc Puskas   9. Tony Barton   10. Jose Altafini

53 *Football League Managers*
1. Ian Greaves   2. Terry Venables   3. Alf Ramsey
(Ipswich Town between 1956/57 and 1961/62)   4. Bill
McCandless   5. Brian Clough (Derby County 1971/72 and
Nottingham Forest 1977/78)   6. Herbert Chapman
(Huddersfield Town 1923/24 and 1924/25 and Arsenal
1930/31 to 1932/33)   7. Bob Stokoe (Blackpool, Bury,
Carlisle United, Rochdale and Sunderland)   8. Wilf
McGuinness   9. Lawrie McMenemy   10. John Lyall (West
Ham United)

54 *National Club Champions, Worldwide*
1. Napoli   2. Anderlecht   3. Dynamo Kiev   4. Linfield
5. Bordeaux   6. Shamrock Rovers   7. Real Madrid
8. Estudiantes   9. Flamenco   10. Inter Milan (1964 and
1965 – beating Independiente of Argentina both times)

55 *World Cup Goalscorers*
1. Gary Lineker 2. Paolo Rossi 3. Laszlo Kiss
4. Robbie Rensenbrink (Holland) 5. Grzegorz Lato
(Poland) 6. Uwe Seeler (West Germany) 7. Teofilo
Cubillas 8. Just Fontaine 9. Sandor Kocsis (Hungary)
10. Ernst Willimowski

56 *Football League—Mixed Bag*
1. Mark Lazarus 2. Plymouth Argyle 3. Nottingham
Forest 4. Leeds United (1968/69) 5. Manchester City
6. Cardiff City 7. Aston Villa 8. Ipswich Town
9. Southport 10. Southampton (Mike Channon)

57 *The Inter-Cities Fairs Cup/European Fairs Cup/*
UEFA Cup – Players
1. John Wark (Ipswich) 2. Trevor Whymark 3. Kevin
Hector 4. Stan Bowles 5. Jupp Heynckes 6. Derek
Dougan 7. Johnny Metgod 8. Bobby Moncur
9. Alfredo di Stefano 10. Sandor Kocsis

58 *Eire Internationals*
1. Ray Houghton 2. Liam Brady 3. Jim Beglin
4. David and Pierce O'Leary 5. Johnny Carey 6. Johnny
Giles 7. Peter Farrell 8. Pat 'Paddy' Mulligan 9. Bill
Whelan 10. Frank O'Farrell

59 *Football League Divisions III and IV*
1. York City 2. Reading 3. Northampton Town
4. Burnley 5. Scarborough 6. Gillingham
7. Wimbledon 8. Preston North End 9. Torquay United
10. Lincoln City

60 *Mixed Bag*
1. Steve Ogrizovic 2. Wayne Harrison 3. Steve
MacKenzie 4. Hugo Sanchez 5. Scot Symon 6. Gordon
Strachan (Aberdeen and Manchester United)
7. Sunderland 8. John Petrie 9. West Bromwich
Albion 10. Dave Cusack

61 *The FA Cup – Giant-killers*
1. Plymouth Argyle 2. York City 3. Walsall
4. Colchester United 5. Swansea Town 6. Mansfield
Town 7. York City 8. Port Vale 9. Norwich City
10. Millwall

62 *England in the Final Stages of the World Cup*
1. Kevin Keegan 2. Trevor Francis, Paul Mariner and
Bryan Robson 3. Jeff Astle 4. Bobby Charlton
5. Johnny Haynes 6. Ron Flowers 7. Tom Finney
8. 1950 9. Chile 10. United States (1950)

63 *Football League Clubs – Mixed Bag*
1. Leeds United 2. Sheffield Wednesday 3. Chelsea
(1954/55) 4. Brentford 5. Manchester City 6. Cardiff
City 7. Wolverhampton Wanderers (1957/58–1960/61)
8. Port Vale 9. Swansea City 10. Huddersfield Town

64 *Record Transfers*
1. Alberto Tarantini 2. Peter Daniel 3. Nicky Johns
4. Arsenal 5. Ian Storey-Moore 6. David Cross 7. Joe
Harper 8. Alex Sabella 9. John Roberts 10. Jimmy
Greaves

65 *The European Cup – Goalscorers*
1. Michel Platini (penalty) 2. Felix Magath 3. John
Robertson 4. Steve Chalmers 5. Ray Crawford 6. Denis
Viollet (Manchester United) 7. Garry Birtles 8. Ferenc
Puskas (1960 against Eintracht Frankfurt and 1962
against Benfica) 9. Gerd Muller (Bayern Munich 1972/
73 and 1973/74) 10. Alfredo di Stefano

66 *Scotland Internationals*
1. George Young 2. Davie Cooper 3. Mark McGhee
4. Asa Hartford 5. Peter Lorimer 6. Denis Law (both
games were at Hampden Park) 7. Bobbie McKinnon
(twenty-eight caps) 8. Hibernian 9. Frank McGarvey
10. David Hay

67 World Cup Managers
1. Enzo Bearzot   2. Walter Winterbottom   3. Cesar Luis Menotti   4. Helmut Schoen   5. Andy Beattie   6. Jose Santamaria   7. Ally Macleod   8. Peter Doherty   9. George Raynor   10. Vittorio Pozzo

68 Football League – One-club Players
1. Jimmy Armfield   2. Nat Lofthouse   3. Harold Bell   4. John Trollope   5. Ron Atkinson   6. Tom Finney   7. Jimmy Dickinson   8. Johnny Haynes   9. Billy Liddell   10. Bob McKinlay

69 England Players
1. Jimmy Mullen   2. Jack and Redfern Froggatt   3. Willie Watson   4. Bill Nicholson   5. Arthur Milton   6. Jack Haines   7. Bedford Jezzard   8. Roger Byrne and Jeff Hall   9. Jimmy Armfield   10. Reg Matthews

70 The Football League Cup/Milk Cup/Littlewoods Cup
1. Clive Allen   2. Arsenal   3. Oxford United   4. Norwich City and Sunderland   5. Liverpool   6. Ron Saunders (Norwich City 1973, Manchester City, 1974, Aston Villa 1975)   7. Nottingham Forest (1978–80)   8. Rochdale in 1962 (losing to Second Division Norwich City 4–0 on aggregate)   9. Birmingham City and Aston Villa   10. Queen's Park Rangers

71 Overseas Players in the Football League
1. Kazimierz Deyna (Poland)   2. Alex Sabella   3. Mirandinha (Newcastle United)   4. Petar Borota   5. Allan Simonsen   6. Bruce Grobbelaar and Craig Johnston   7. John Chiedozie   8. Ivan Golac   9. Radimir Antic   10. Frans Thijssen (Ipswich Town)

72 Brazil in the World Cup
1. Careca   2. Paolo Rossi (Italy)   3. Carlos Alberto   4. Mario Zagalo   5. Didi   6. Jairzinho   7. Garrincha   8. Vava   9. Pele   10. Hungary

73 *The European Cup Winners' Cup – Mixed Bag*
1. Arsenal (lost on penalties in 1980)   2. Sporting Lisbon
3. Chelsea (1971/72 against Jeunesse Hautcharage)
4. Glasgow Rangers (1961 and 1967)   5. Manchester
United   6. Tottenham Hotspur (1963)
7. Wolverhampton Wanderers   8. Dynamo Moscow
9. Ian Bowyer   10. Paul Vaessen

74 *The FA Cup – Players*
1. Ray Clemence (Liverpool 1971, 1974 and 1977;
Tottenham Hotspur 1982 and 1987)   2. Pat Rice
(Arsenal, 1971, 1972, 1978, 1979 and 1980)   3. Pat
Jennings (Tottenham Hotspur 1967; Arsenal 1978, 1979
and 1980)   4. Manchester United (1963)   5. Ernie Taylor
(Newcastle United 1951, Blackpool 1953 and Manchester
United 1958)   6. Stan Crowther (1957 – Aston Villa
against Manchester United, 1958 – Manchester United
against Bolton Wanderers)   7. Raich Carter (Sunderland
1937 and Derby County 1946)   8. Willie Fagan   9. Dave
Mackay   10. Bob Barclay

75 *Leading Football League Goalscorers in One Season*
1. Terry Bly   2. Kerry Dixon (with Reading in the first
season, then with Chelsea)   3. Clive Allen (playing for
Queen's Park Rangers)   4. Mick Walsh and Bob Hatton
5. West Bromwich Albion (Johnny Nicholls : tied with
Huddersfield's Jim Glazzard – and Ronnie Allen; Jeff Astle
and Tony Brown)   6. Derek Dooley   7. Gary Lineker
(Leicester City 1984/85 – jointly with Kerry Dixon – and
Everton 1985/86)   8. Ray Crawford (Ipswich Town)
9. Jimmy Greaves (Chelsea 1960/61)   10. Ronnie Rooke

76 *England Players with One Cap*
1. Danny Wallace   2. Brian Little   3. Colin Harvey
4. John Hollins   5. Ken Brown   6. George Robb
7. Nigel Spink   8. Peter Ward   9. Alan Sunderland
10. Brian Stein

77 Scottish Football
1. Hearts 2. Rangers 3. Frank McGarvey 4. Gary Gillespie 5. Hamish McAlpine (Dundee United goalkeeper) 6. Raith Rovers 7. Jim Bone 8. Paul Hegarty 9. Hamilton Academicals 10. Jimmy McGrory

78 1986/87—Mixed Bag
1. Exeter City 2. Mark Dennis (Southampton against Aston Villa) 3. Igor Belanov (USSR) 4. Jan Molby (Liverpool) 5. River Plate (Argentina) 6. Terry Butcher 7. Tom and Tony English 8. Chris Waddle 9. John Aldridge 10. Mark Higgins

79 Football League – Multi-club Players
1. Peter Shilton (Leicester, Stoke, Nottingham Forest, Southampton, and now Derby County) 2. Colin Garwood 3. Tony McNamara 4. Alan Durban 5. Kevin Bremner 6. Tommy Briggs 7. John O'Rourke 8. Chris Jones (Manchester City, Swindon Town, Oldham Athletic, Walsall, York City, Huddersfield Town, Doncaster Rovers, Darlington, and Rochdale) 9. Fred Pickering 10. Charlie Wayman

80 Transfer Trail
1. Teddy Maybank 2. Don Masson 3. Gary Collier 4. Asa Hartford 5. Roger Davies 6. John (Dixie) Deans 7. John McClelland 8. Ray Houghton 9. George Best 10. Richard Money

81 The Inter-cities Fairs Cup/European Fairs Cup/ UEFA Cup – Mixed Bag
1. John Wark (Ipswich 1980/81) 2. Leeds United 3. Barcelona 4. Tottenham Hotspur 5. Feyenoord 6. Valencia 7. Kevin Keegan 8. Wolverhampton Wanderers 9. London 10. Leeds United

82 World Cup—Mixed Bag
1. Bobby and Jack Charlton 2. Bernd and Karl-Heinz Forster 3. Rene and Willy Van der Kerkhof 4. Scotland (1974) 5. Brazil 6. Dino Zoff (Italy) 7. Grzegorz Lato (Poland) 8. North Korea 9. Cameroon 10. Tunisia

83 *Scots Managers in England*
1. Sir Matt Busby   2. Bill Shankly   3. Tommy Docherty
4. Billy Bremner   5. George Graham   6. Jimmy Sirrel
7. Dave Mackay   8. Dally Duncan   9. Ian Porterfield
10. Portsmouth

84 *The European Championships*
1. USSR   2. Henri Delauney   3. Spain (beating the
USSR in Madrid)   4. Scotland   5. 1968 (in Italy)   6. Italy
(beating Yugoslavia in 1968)   7. West Germany
8. Gunter Netzer   9. Wales   10. Italy

85 *Mixed Bag*
1. Tranmere Rovers   2. Brian Lloyd   3. Chris Woods
4. Ian Callaghan (Liverpool)   5. Steve Galliers   6. Robbie
James (Swansea City)   7. Tony Knapp   8. Eoin Hand
9. Mark Wright (Southampton against Liverpool)
10. Bobby Moore

86 *The FA Cup Goalscorers*
1. Roger Osborne (Ipswich Town against Arsenal in
1978)   2. Alan Taylor   3. Steve Heighway (1971 and
1974, both times for Liverpool)   4. Bryan Robson
(Manchester United)   5. Bobby Johnstone   6. Don Revie
7. Doug Holden (Bolton Wanderers and Preston North End)
and Alex Dawson (Manchester United and Preston North
End)   8. Ted MacDougall (AFC Bournemouth)   9. Noel
Kinsey   10. Stan Mortensen (1948 and 1953, both times
for Blackpool)

87 *Football League Players*
1. Frank Clark   2. John Hickton   3. Tommy Tynan
4. Steve Whitworth   5. Wally Ardron (217 goals between
1946 and 1954)   6. Les Mutrie   7. Alan Mullery (Fulham
and Tottenham Hotspur)   8. Geoff Vowden   9. Bill
Foulkes   10. Chris Nicholl

88 Wales and Northern Ireland in the Final Stages of the World Cup

1. Norman Whiteside 2. Gerry Armstrong 3. Mal Donaghy 4. Peter McParland 5. Czechoslovakia
6. Danny Blanchflower 7. John and Mel Charles
8. Hungary 9. Ivor Allchurch 10. Jack Kelsey

89 The European Cup – Clubs

1. Anderlecht (Belgium) 2. Porto (Portugal) 3. Dundee United 4. Juventus 5. Nottingham Forest 6. Red Star Belgrade 7. Manchester City 8. Manchester United
9. Benfica 10. Ipswich (in the preliminary round of the 1963 competition) against Floriana of Malta

90 Internationals – Mixed Bag

1. Johnny Carey (Manchester United) 2. Dr Kevin and Michael O'Flanagan 3. Gary Owen 4. Terry Venables
5. Arsenal – Leslie Compton and Ray Daniel 6. Vic Rouse (Crystal Palace) 7. Viv Anderson (Nottingham Forest)
8. Danny Blanchflower (Northern Ireland) 9. Stan Mortensen 10. George Hardwick

91 Long-serving Football League Players

1. John McGovern 2. Alan Oakes 3. Scunthorpe United 4. Frank Worthington 5. David Webb
6. Portsmouth 7. Charlton Athletic (ninety-five League games 1964–67) 8. Phil Boyer 9. Frank Large
10. Peter Noble

92 Record Transfers

1. Steve Archibald (Aberdeen) 2. Wyn Davies 3. Peter Withe 4. Alan Hunter, Paul Mariner and Kevin O'Callaghan 5. Kevin Hird 6. Mick Robinson (Preston North End) 7. David Hay (Glasgow Celtic) 8. John Hawley, Stan Cummins and Claudio Marangoni 9. Bruce Rioch 10. Alan Curbishley

93 *England Players*
1. Jim Langley   2. Eddie Clamp and Bill Slater   3. Warren Bradley   4. Tommy Taylor   5. Eddie Holliday   6. Joe Baker   7. Frank Wignall   8. Norman Hunter   9. Tommy Smith and Larry Lloyd   10. Mick Mills and Frank Lampard

94 *World Cup—Mixed Bag*
1. Ferenc Puskas   2. Jose 'Mazzola' Altafini   3. Luisito Monti   4. Sweden   5. Hungary (4–2 in the semi-final) 6. The Maracana Stadium, Rio de Janeiro (1950)   7. Jules Rimet   8. George Robledo   9. Wladislaw Zmuda 10. Norman Whiteside (Northern Ireland, 1982)

95 *Football League—Mixed Bag*
1. Coventry City   2. Bill Nicholson (Tottenham Hotspur, 1951 and 1961)   3. Arsenal   4. Tommy Lawton 5. Middlesbrough   6. Hartlepool United   7. Jimmy Greaves   8. Dixie Dean   9. Peter Ward   10. Ivor Broadis

96 *International Players Worldwide*
1. Morten Olsen   2. Bjorn Nordquist   3. Oleg Blokhin 4. Paul van Himst   5. Ernst Ocwirk   6. Anton Ondrus 7. Berti Vogts   8. Roberto Rivelino   9. Hector Chumpitaz   10. Giacinto Facchetti

97 *European Competitions – Mixed Bag*
1. Terry McDermott   2. Ray Kennedy (Arsenal 1970, Liverpool 1976)   3. Denis Law (Manchester United 1964/65 and 1968/69)   4. Juventus   5. Liverpool (1975/76 and 1976/77)   6. Ajax, Amsterdam   7. Leeds United   8. Ian Callaghan and Tommy Smith (Cup Winners' Cup 1966, UEFA Cup 1973 and 1976, European Cup 1977)   9. England   10. Aberdeen (1983)

98 *World Cup Referees and Linesmen*
1. R. Arppi Filho   2. Jack Taylor   3. Clive Thomas 4. Georg Dienst   5. Rudolf Kreitlein   6. Jim Finney 7. Ken Aston   8. Mervyn Griffiths   9. Arthur Ellis 10. Jean Langenus

99 FA Cup—Mixed Bag
1. Stamford Bridge (1920–22) 2. Joe Mercer 3. Billy Walker 4. Bill Slater (Wolverhampton Wanderers, 1960) 5. Stoke City 6. Leeds United 7. Walter Hampson 8. Brian Kidd 9. Nottingham Forest 10. Arsenal (1970/71 and 1971/72)

100 Football League Clubs – Expert
1. Blackpool 2. Bristol City 3. Leicester City 4. Port Vale 5. Wolverhampton Wanderers 6. Fulham 7. AFC Bournemouth (then Bournemouth and Boscombe Athletic) 8. Oldham Athletic 9. Aldershot 10. Wolverhampton Wanderers

101 1988 – International Matches
1. Mick Harford 2. Tony Adams 3. Colombia 4. Tony Dorigo (Chelsea) 5. Wales (goal by Ian Rush) 6. Ray Houghton 7. Marco van Basten 8. Bryan Robson (vs Holland); Tony Adams (vs USSR) 9. Morton Olsen (Denmark) 10. Igor Belanov (USSR)

102 1988 – Cup Competitions
1. Lawrie Sanchez (Wimbledon) 2. Sutton United 3. Everton and Sheffield Wednesday 4. Trevor Senior 5. Port Vale 6. Dunfermline Athletic 7. Reading 8. Steve Francis 9. Nigel Winterburn (Arsenal) 10. Pieter Den Boer

103 1988 – Mixed Bag
1. Mark Walters 2. PSV Eindhoven (drew 1–1 with Twente Enschede) 3. Gary Bailey 4. Ian Ferguson (Glasgow Rangers) 5. Laurie Cunningham (Wimbledon, previously for Real Madrid, European Cup, 1980/81) 6. Dave Caldwell (Torquay) 7. Garry Pallister (Middlesbrough) 8. David Williams 9. Jim Leighton (Aberdeen to Manchester United, Dave Beasant (Wimbledon to Newcastle United) 10. Gordon Cowans (returns to Aston Villa from Bari)